FREUD

FREUD

Knowing and
Not Wanting
to Know

Fredric Larry Weiss

ST. MARTIN'S PRESS   NEW YORK

Acknowledgment is made for permission to reprint from the following material.

From *The Interpretation of Dreams*, by Sigmund Freud. Translated from the German and edited by James Strachey. Published in the United States by Basic Books, Inc., by arrangement with George Allen & Unwin Ltd. and the Hogarth Press, Ltd. Reprinted by permission of Basic Books, Inc., and George Allen & Unwin Ltd.

From *Studies on Hysteria*, by Josef Breuer and Sigmund Freud. Translated from the German and edited by James Strachey in collaboration with Anna Freud, assisted by Alix Strachey and Alan Tyson. Published in the United States by Basic Books, Inc., by arrangement with the Hogarth Press, Ltd. Reprinted by permission of Basic Books, Inc.

From *The Standard Edition of the Complete Psychological Works of Sigmund Freud*. Translated and edited by James Strachey. Reprinted by permission of Sigmund Freud Copyrights, the Institute of Psycho-Analysis, and the Hogarth Press, Ltd.

First published in the United States of America in 1990

Printed in the United States of America

Designed by Judy Dannecker

Library of Congress Cataloging-in-Publication Data

Weiss, Fredric Larry.
    Freud: knowing and not wanting to know.
        p.   cm.
    Includes bibliographical references.
    ISBN 0-312-04567-0
    1. Psychoanalysis.   2. Freud, Sigmund, 1856–1939.   I. Title.
8F173.W422   1990   150.19'52—dc20   89-78310

To Cecelia,
Louella, H.B.,
Peggy, and Josh

CONTENTS

Preface

I have a relationship with Freud's ideas that goes back almost thirty years. I remember when my first tutor Merrill Rodin, casually handed me some of Freud's writing and said he thought I might enjoy reading Freud. From then on, sometimes more focused, sometimes less, Freud's ideas have affected me the way, according to Plato, lovers should be affected by those who loved them: he impregnated my soul. I hope this has led to some wisdom. This book reflects some of the pleasure Freud has given me, even in disagreement.

I would like to acknowledge some of those people who are somewhere in this book: Merrill Rodin, Harold Zyskind, Bob Creeley, and Sy Rochlin. I want to especially thank Richard Wollheim for his encouragement and support. Over many years, I have discussed my ideas on Freud with him. In particular, it was his criticisms of some of my earlier views which led me to develop the cognitive dimensions in Freud. Also, I want to especially thank Priscilla Trowbridge. She stayed up many nights discussing this material with me. Her patience, as well as her ability to understand what I was doing and her grace, were pillars of support never forgotten.

FREUD

INTRODUCTION

This book is a close reading of Freud. It brings to the fore the phenomenological implications of resistance as well as the cognitive dimensions of Freud's work; in doing this, it makes explicit what is implicit in Freud. Unlike Freud's official theories, which center around the vicissitudes of affective ideas and later derivatives—infantile wishes, component instincts, libido; that is, hypothetical or supposed real components of a person or psyche—the explanation I develop centers around a person, what the person does, and the meaning of the person's actions. What I put forward as Freud's working in-practice theory is implicit in Freud, mostly revealed in case history material.

My analysis does not rely on contemporary theories or models developed in psychoanalysis, nor on biographical material. Nor do I attempt to psychoanalyze Freud or any of his patients. It is clear, however, that Freud had difficulty reconciling his chronicles of case material with his ideas of being a man of science. Freud was committed by training and desire to reductionistic explanations and theories which modeled the type of explanations offered in the natural sciences. From this perspective everything "complex" is to be reduced to the smallest item or ingredient with the hope that laws of cohesion and development can be established. These assumptions in conjunction with Freud's neurological/medical training directed his overall theoretical approach. Whether Freud was investigating hysteria, dreams, or slips of the tongue, his questions and formulations focused around etiology, specific causal determination, mechanisms of formation, choice of illness, or specific dream expression. Most of Freud's theories approach the material of observation from one of these perspectives or attempt to provide an overall link to all of these categories. We shall see how Freud's theoretical inclinations led him to formulations that obscured what he was doing and accomplishing.

At the same time, Freud was also what I would call an intuitive empiricist with the instincts of a bloodhound. His case material reveals an investigator not hemmed in by his own theoretical proclamations—nor, at times, overly concerned with what he sometimes referred to as his "looseness of phraseology." Under this euphemism, descriptive material could slip in through theoretical back doors that contradicted the very theoretical formulations the material was presented to illustrate.

As I said, this book is a close reading of Freud. My analysis is primarily a textual examination that develops the implicit logic of what he is presenting. I examine theoretical claims on the grounds in which they are presented; I examine case history material as he presents and uses it to illustrate theoretical claims. When I depart or diverge from Freud's theoretical conclusions, my differences are based on the material Freud is presenting. It will be clear that right from the beginning his theoretical assumptions lead him in one direction and his case material in another, and this latter direction will lead to explanations that are neither reductionistic or causal.

This book is my attempt to return our thinking to the ideas and problems Freud was addressing. It is my attempt to recapture the excitement of Freud and experience the paradoxical quality of his investigations. In a relatively short period of time, Freud's theories have traveled from oblivion and scorn to more or less accepted clichés. When I have taught courses on

Freud I have had to contend with a bewildering range of pre-conception about the meaning of Freud's central concepts and just as bewildering a range of responses to these preconceptions. I am continually faced with the frustrating situation of attempting to teach what so many claim to already know. However, when I am successful, and people do try to read Freud, many are surprised and delighted to find how far removed Freud is from the clichés that surround him. I do not think the situation is that much better with my colleagues in psychology, and my fellow psychotherapists and psychoanalysts. The reasons are different and more complex, but I have never met so many people who have so many views that are so far removed from the person they claim to be so influenced by.

I want to return to Freud. I will be bringing to the fore much of the material that Freud confused or obscured in his theoretical formulations. I want the reader to experience—as if anew—the outrage, delight, frustration, and confusion of Freud's thinking. I want readers to be intrigued with Elisabeth von R. and the Rat Man and hear their stories and feel their dilemmas. I ask readers to try and lay aside, as much as possible, their preconceptions and allow themselves to digest, through untangled material, that curious state of mind that Freud was referring to when using terms (that have now become hackneyed) like "unconscious." I also want the reader to understand the theoretical foundations of Freud's work: how it guides his thinking, how he creates substantial theories from limited concepts, how he incorporates and fits new material into old formulations, both how he was theoretically marooned in the past and how his curiosity led him to transcend his own views.

In *The Interpretation of Dreams,* Freud argued that he could use a child's dream and its interpretation to demonstrate the logic and meaning of adult dreams. The advantage of the child's dream was in its clarity and in the transparency of what it revealed. Adult dreams had a similar meaning, function, and nuclear core but were more necessarily complex, confused, and distorted. In a similar manner, I argue that Freud's thinking in the *Studies of Hysteria* and in his key papers on "The Neuro-Psychoses of Defense" reveal in a transparent form assumptions, insights, and confusions that are incorporated in and become necessarily obscured in the complexity of Freud's later mature theories. Beginning with Breuer's case of Anna O. and its use in the "Preliminary Communication" (which becomes the first chapter in the *Studies on Hysteria*) and through close analysis of Freud's most developed case history in the *Studies,* the case of Elisabeth von R., I closely follow how his theory works in practice and what the material of observation is revealing. Between the *Studies on Hysteria* and *The Interpretation of Deams* Freud's theories and observations become much more complex. I indicate what some of this new material is, chart the development of Freud's wish-fulfillment theories, and show how they are continuations of, and incorporate original assumptions and misconceptions of, his earlier views. My primary concern, however, is to bring out as clearly as possible Freud's mature working explanation of neurosis. With that in mind I closely examine the case of the Rat Man, utilizing and arguing against the strongest version of the wish-fulfillment theory as a means to fully develop the implications of this extraordinary case history.

I believe separating Freud's insights from his theoretical confusions allows the material of observation to emerge, revealing the logic of its own explanation.

1. THE BEGINNING

In 1893, Freud, in collaboration with Josef Breuer, published a paper under the title "On the Psychical Mechanism of Hysterical Phenomena."[1] This paper indicated the conceptual framework within which Freud and Breuer began their work, outlined their initial theory of the etiology and cure of hysteria (which centered around the concept, originally Breuer's, of "abreaction"), and briefly described the form of therapy that the authors used.

The paper was republished in 1895 as the introductory chapter—the "Preliminary Communication"—in *Studies in Hysteria*,[2] which was jointly published by Freud and Breuer, and contained also five short case histories (including that of Breuer's patient Anna O., whose case had first led him to form the concept of "abreaction" in hysteria), a theoretical chapter by Breuer, and one on therapy by Freud.

1. By "reaction" we here understand the whole class of voluntary and involuntary reflexes—in which, as experience shows us, the affects are discharged. If this reaction takes place to a sufficient amount a large part of the affect disappears as a result. Linguistic usage bears witness to

this fact of daily observation by such phrases as "to cry oneself out," and "to blow off steam."[3]

She played restlessly with her fingers . . . or rubbed her hands against one another . . . so as to prevent herself from screaming. This person reminds one forcibly of one of the principles laid down by Darwin to explain the expression of emotions—the principle of the overflow of excitation, which accounts, for instance, for dogs wagging their tails.[4]

For Freud and Breuer, as they began to investigate and treat neurosis, the overflow of affect or excitation was not just one of the principles that explained emotional reaction. Emotional reactions were conceived of as invariably being (or accomplishing) such an overflow, and this concept was, as Breuer said, "fundamental to our theme."[5] The authors pictured reactions such as weeping in sorrow or breaking things in rage, and actions such as undergoing confessions or committing an act of revenge, as relieving the subject of his emotion or feeling ("affect") by pouring it out or using it up. Affect was conceived of as a quantity, almost a substance. Theoretically, the authors found a relevant distinction between one emotion (they said, "sum of effect") and another not in terms of the name it could be given—e.g., sorrow, rage, guilt—but solely in terms of its amount. And, theoretically, they conceived of all emotional reactions and many actions as having the same reason and effect—to discharge a sum of affect that, because it was excessive, had been oppressing the subject. A reaction would relieve the subject of his excess of affect if it were sufficient in duration or intensity. If it were not vehement or prolonged enough, too much affect would remain, and the subject would continue to be oppressed by his disgust, fear, or vengefulness.

It seemed to follow that, for the fundamental purpose, any reaction would be precisely as good as another of the same magnitude. In fact Freud and Breuer used examples such as that of Frau Emmy von N., who played with her hands to keep from screaming, to substantiate the view of affect as a quantity requiring discharge when great and of emotional reaction as constituting its discharge. Breuer cited a story told of Bismarck—angry at the King, but constrained not to show his feelings before the ruler, he smashed a valuable vase—and explained it as follows: the "excitation of anger," denied discharge in the most obvious or normal manner, was "transposed" to an alternative reaction. "We feel relieved provided it is used up by *any* strong motor innervation."[6]

As I said, Freud and Breuer pictured emotional reactions as an overflow of affect *or* (nervous) excitation. They conceived of nervous excitation as a physical correlate or analogue of affect, but it was never simply a matter of their drawing a parallel between what could be said of excitation and what of emotion (affect). Their concept of "cranial excitation" was modeled on a concept of affect. It was based, in the first instance, on such common cases as those the authors cited, in which a person could be said to be relieved of emotion through expression, reaction, or action. Everything they thought affect did, they pictured excitation as doing: if affect increased, so did excitation; if affect was thought to be dammed up (through lack of proper reaction), so was excitation; affect was supposed to be connected with certain ideas, and excitation to be attached to or spring from the neurological correlates of those ideas. That is, they conceived of each sum of affect as springing from or being attached, until discharge, to an idea—paradigmatically, the memory of an event. (For instance, an amount of fear would be connected with the memory of an accident.) And in the central nervous system, a unit corresponding to the mental unit would correspondingly be occupied by a charge of nervous excitation.

But if their neurological picture was based on a view of what was "psychical," the reverse was also true—nervous excitation left its mark on affect. Affect was emotion viewed as something to which excitation was analogous. If it was emotion, in the first instance, of which a person could be said to be relieved through reaction or expression, it was nervous excitation, in

7

the first instance, that could be imagined to flow away or be used up in "motor innervations."[7]

2. Between 1880 and 1882, Breuer treated a hysterical woman he called Anna O. Among many others, she suffered from the following symptoms: contractions and anesthesia of the limbs; deafness in certain circumstances; disturbances of the eyes, such as a convergent squint, and of vision, such as macropsia and inability to focus on more than one object at a time; hallucinations and "negative hallucinations" such as being unable to see or recognize people who came to see her; and inability to speak or even to understand her native language, and substitution of another for it. (At one time, if she were given a text in French to read aloud, what she would produce, without realizing it, would be an excellent extempore English translation.)

Also, at one point in her illness, she spent a great deal of time throwing pillows about, and at another she would run off to climb a tree in the midst of a conversation.

When Breuer first saw Anna O., she alternated between a comparatively normal condition and a sort of twilight state, in which she cried out "tormenting, tormenting." Breuer found that if he questioned her when she was in this condition, she would tell him distressing stories. Anna in her more normal condition was aware that she did fall into a *"condition seconde"* (she invented a name for it—"clouds"), that in it she told Breuer something that was troubling her, and that having talked to him seemed to soothe her and bring about a general improvement in her illness. But she was unaware of what it was that she told Breuer. When the "talking cure," as she called it, had to be put off because of Breuer's absence, she became worse again, and her behavior deteriorated. When Breuer returned, he had to listen to even more stories than usual. Anna then instituted a development of the therapeutic procedure: in her *"condition seconde"* she started to tell Breuer of the circumstances in which her symptoms had originated. When she told him of these events, expressing much distress over them, she was not only soothed, but her symptoms began to disappear. Breuer began to get the same results by hypnotizing the patient and asking her when she had developed a certain symptom. (For instance, she had suffered for some time from an inability to drink. Under hypnosis she told Breuer, with the expression of great disgust, how she had seen an unpleasant little dog belonging to her hired companion drink from a glass. Anna then called for water and woke from hypnosis with the glass at her lips. The symptom did not return.)

Picturing the "talking cure" as an overflow of affect, Freud and Breuer arrived at "abreaction" or "catharsis": a hysteric gives vehement expression to affect connected with a certain idea or memory, which previously was ostensibly forgotten, or "split off" from normal consciousness, and in doing so is relieved, not only of affect, but also of a symptom.[8] The authors made this the center of a view of hysteria. The patient had a symptom because there had previously been no adequate discharge. A large amount of affect had been "strangulated"; that is, it had been unable to find a normal way out through reaction, expression, or "associative correction."[9] In a person with a particular predisposition, a "strangulated" amount of affect might bring about a hysterical symptom. Two factors could be made to account for the bottling-up. Either the patient had been in a "hypnoid state" when a traumatic event occurred (in which case, reaction was impossible, and the memory of the event was "split off" from normal consciousness),[10] or the patient had met such an event with no overt reaction, but only with an "effort of defense"; that is, an attempt to put the event out of mind, or treat it as *"non-arrivee,"* in consequences of which the memory would not be genuinely forgotten, but instead become unconsious. In either case, what prevented discharge when the event occurred also made the idea unconscious, or "split off," and hence prevented an adequate discharge after the event. The idea thus became "pathogenic."[11]

The lack of discharge supposedly explained not only why an amount of affect was bottled up, but also why the idea with which it was connected could remain for an indefinite period unconscious or split off rather than being gradually forgotten, as distressing memories generally are. A man who has been in an accident forgets the event in time when, through reaction or "associative correction," he has ceased to feel fearful about it; before it can be normally "worn away," an idea must become "weak" by the removal of the affect connected with it.

In short, Freud's and Breuer's initial theory of hysteria was that hysterical symptoms occur because the large amounts of affect have remained undischarged; they have lacked discharge because the ideas with which they are connected have been split off from normal consciousness (by hypnoid states or acts of defense); the symptoms can be cured if the patient can be brought to recall the split-off ideas and give verbal expression to the dammed-up affect.

3. The overflow of emotional reaction was used to reduce every case in which a person could be said to be "relieved of emotion" to the same factors. It would direct attention exclusively to questions of quantity: the strength or weakness of an emotion (or its "amount"), the presence or absence of an overt reaction, the vehemence and length of whatever reaction there may have been (or *its* "amount").

It would seem, then, to exclude from consideration any question of what the emotion was in a particular case, why the subject felt as he did, why he performed *this* reaction or action and not another, or why his emotion was something of which he could be relieved and should have been relieved, and to exclude any other answer than that of quantity to the question of why the subject was relieved of emotion through expression. (The concept of affect as a quantity that is discharged in expression or reaction leaves it a mystery, for instance, that one neither does get rid of joy through expression, nor would be better off if he did; that a man may grow angrier as he pounds the table, without being provoked; and that a dying Christian might or might not be relieved of a lifetime's feeling, or conviction, of guilt by the merest token of a confession, if it were conveyed to a priest who gave him absolution.)

Freud and Breuer accepted the overflow picture as literally correct. They accepted it as an explanation of the occurrence and efficacy of a bout of weeping, for instance, or an act of revenge, that the reaction served to discharge excessive affect (or excitation); they did not consider "discharge" a metaphor, but thought it a "fact of daily observation," confirmed by linguistic usage.

But some of what the fundamental concept took away in theory it gave back in practice: some of the questions that it was the purpose of the overflow picture to exclude as irrelevant were implicit in it, from its inception.

A. The view of affect as a quantity discharged in reactions was based on cases in which some specific emotion (e.g., anger, fear, sorrow) was expressed and overcome: so to begin with, an affect was considered not just as a quantity of steam, but as a *specific* quantity of steam, distinguishable from others in terms of its name, object, or occasion. (One's fear over an accident would be considered a different quantity from one's fear of old age.)

B. The overflow picture was based on cases in which some specifiable emotion was expressed and overcome, generally through the form of action or reaction that Breuer termed a "pre-formed reflex": so from the beginning affects were considered as specific, distinct quantities of steam, each of which had its own appropriate ways of being let off.

4. The nonquantitative assumptions already present in the picture of affect as a quantity, discharged in emotional reaction, were reflected and enlarged in the framework that was built up around affective ideas—strangulation and abreaction.

A. The concept of an *"affective idea"* was an attempt to reduce something like a memory of a frightening accident to factors essential for its explanation on the "psychical" level—a unitary idea, a quantum of affect—and at the same time to make it easily translatable into the neurological shadow-picture. But it should be noted that one cannot speak of any "affective ideas" without at least bringing into consideration the nature of a specific emotion, distinct from others (*an* affect, not just a sum of affect), and its object or occasion.

B. The concept of nonexpression as lack of discharge or *strangulation* was an attempt to isolate one factor to explain the formation of hysterical symptoms, and to relate this factor to the explanation of oppression by emotion in general.

Freud and Breuer believed that a strangulated sum of affect (or its brother cranial excitation) was the immediate cause of a hysterical symptom. This precise formulation was, however, a point of ambiguity, and it allowed further equivocation. For instance, Freud, at a rather late date, explained a failure in cathartic therapy ostensibly in quantitative terms, to wit: it takes more than this feeble effort on the part of the therapist to rid a hysteric of her powerful *idees fixes*.[12] Note that he does not say that not enough of the load of affect has been expressed, but that the *idea* is too strong.

Freud wrote—indeed, at a later date than the "Preliminary Communication"—that it is a "question of how much affective tension . . . an organism can tolerate."[13] But in conformity with the concept of affective ideas, Freud and Breuer considered a hysteric to be suffering not just from a total quantity of undischarged affect, but from specifiable amounts (plural) of affect, identifiable as the emotions she finally expresses over ostensibly forgotten events.

Freud and Breuer held that one is distressed by a sum of affect because it is a large amount and has not been expressed. And their fundamental concept leaves unanswerable such questions as why one does not rid oneself of happiness or devotion by expressing it, nor would be better off if one did. Yet in practice Freud and Breuer seem to have assumed that affects that distress a person are distressing affects; the affective ideas they sought were memories of frightening, disgusting, or sad events.

One way of formulating the relationship between a strangulated sum of affect (or affective ideas) and a hysterical symptom was to call the symptom an abnormal expression of emotion. But it never occurred to Freud and Breuer to wonder why a symptom were not self-curing if it were continued for a long time, nor to wonder why, in any case, the postulated excess of affect were not removed by abnormal behavior, such as throwing pillows about.

Freud may have taken the "expression of emotion" formulation as a sort of metaphor, thinking it more correct to say that a sum of affect (or excitation) produces a cause, as by pressing on a nerve, but when he undertook to answer the question why *this* symptom occurs and not another, his attempts in this direction always were concerned with the nature of a specific "affective idea." The practice of therapy was evidently directing him toward this kind of answer: consider the example of Anna O. and the glass of water.

C. The concept of expression or reaction as discharge, pouring out or using up, *abreaction,* was intended to isolate the central factor in the explanation of the cure of hysterical symptoms, and to identify this factor with the explanation of relief from emotion in general. Together with the theory of mobility—which Breuer stated in explaining Bismarck's vase-smashing as the theory that any form of expression or reaction of sufficient length and intensity can take the place of the natural or normal outlet: "we feel relieved provided (the sum of affect or excitation) is used up in *any* strong motor innervation"[14]—abreaction could be made to account for the function and success of the cathartic therapy and, in certain formulations, for the occurrence of hysterical symptoms.

Freud and Breuer again accepted these concepts as literally correct; Breuer, for instance, thought not only that they provided a correct explanation of Bismarck's smashing the vase, but that there was nothing else to be said about the incident.

In their practice of therapy, their attention was directed to ideas as vehicles of sums of affect that had to be discharged. Accordingly, having located an affective idea that a patient had failed to get rid of in the natural or normal manner, they were concerned only to effect a delayed discharge through verbal expression, and inquired no further about the idea or emotion;

for instance, to consider why Anna O. had been so very disgusted to see a dog drink from a glass.

They did not consider the therapist to be one who helps a patient to cease being disgusted over certain past happenings or to overcome certain fears, but as one who performs an operation to "extirpate" a "foreign body." Accordingly, they carried out the operation while the patient was under hypnosis, and they tried to make sure that the expression of affect was sufficiently vehement and prolonged. It was considered best that the patient should not be aware, when returned to a normal state, of what had taken place.

Sometimes too they would try to hasten the wearing-away of the idea by employing posthypnotic suggestion against it, once its affect had been discharged. On the one hand, this factor of practice was in accordance with the view of therapy as mental surgery. But on the other hand, it again reflects the ambiguity implicit in the statement that the patient suffers from strangulated affective ideas; if it was the lack of discharge of affect that produced a symptom, why should the vehicle idea itself be treated as "pathogenic"? And, indeed, why should the affect have to be expressed in connection with the idea?

The mobility theory itself, as I have already said, gave back in practice some of the nonquantitative considerations that it seemed to be excluding by introducing a natural or normal form of discharge for a particular emotion. Breuer made this a point of ambiguity, allowing further equivocation, by using the term "adequate" in two senses: an adequate reaction was either a normal expression or "pre-formed reflex," or any reaction of sufficient amount to use up the excess of affect.

Indeed, as Freud and Breuer put the mobility theory into practice with their cathartic therapy, all its central terms—"adequate," "expression" or "reaction," "relief"—had many meanings. That is, in the theory that, for the universal purpose of relief from emotion, any expression or reaction of sufficient duration and vehemence may replace the "pre-formed reflex"; "expression or reaction" seems to be a general term (cf. "discharge"). "Expression or reaction" also applies to what Freud and Breuer had their patients do toward relief from emotion and symptom. But what they had a patient do was not *any* thing that would ordinarily express and/or bring relief from emotion (e.g., hitting someone, throwing things, singing). Instead, the patient was made to recall events and to express emotion over them in the sense in which one expresses one's anger by talking of what made one angry, and how angry one feels—perhaps with weeping and gnashing of teeth, but not with blows and acts of revenge. This was not, then, expression-in-general, but a cross between telling one's feelings to a confidant (who, perhaps, elicits an account of emotions one did not know one had) and confessing them, as to a priest (who, aside from the eliciting function, has also the capacity of granting absolution). The form of expression or delayed reaction or discharge that Freud and Breuer utilized in practice happened somehow to be a form that often is "adequate" to bring about some "relief" in emotional matters, although its adequacy in general is not directly related to its amount, and although to say "we feel relieved" is not necessarily the same as saying that we are relieved of the emotion that has been expressed.

5. The fundamental concept of affect (quantity and discharge) seemed to have the advantage of isolating the central factors for explaining any case of emotional reaction (identifying the factors in any given case with those in any other) and of permitting a translation of "psychical" factors into the terms of "cranial excitation." This apparent advantage was undoubtedly of considerable influence in maintaining, as well as formulating, the concept, for in hysterical symptoms Freud and Breuer had to deal with evidently physical phenomena, which seemed to require an explanation in terms of causes, neurological as well as emotional. But the fundamental concept of affect was an uneasy compromise between emotion and excitation. The factors it isolated as essential for explanation were neither the factors essential for an explanation of emotion, expression, and relief, nor neurological factors at all.

The fundamental concept, and the framework of affective ideas, strangulation, and abreaction, had the apparent advantage of specificity (as to the central factors and the relations among them) and of radical limitation or reduction. But in its very inception (in application to ordinary cases of emotional expression or reaction) it admitted—as it were, through the back door—considerations that it ostensibly eliminated. It proved loose enough to permit considerations and assumptions concerning, for instance, specific "ideas" and disturbing emotions to be introduced without being recognized as alien. Finally, put into practice in the investigation and treatment of cases of hysteria—even such a case as Anna O., which gave rise to the theory of abreaction, and all the phenomena of which seemed comprehensible in themselves and as related to one another only in terms of the quantitative framework—it permitted distinctions to be made that were antithetical to the conceptual framework but could be made in its terms, so that they seemed to conform perfectly to it. Thus in practice the framework of affective ideas, strangulation, abreaction, lost its apparent advantage of specificity and limitation and took on something of a contrary advantage—of looseness and flexibility of application. But this was certainly a dubious advantage; on the one hand, the capacity of the quantitative terminology for ambiguity and equivocation allowed Freud to do what his theory would appear not to allow him to do, but on the other hand, it allowed him to accept a theory that, from the very beginning, could not account for his material of observation and practice of therapy—that, even in the case of Anna O., was contradicted by his observation and practice.

2. HYPOTHESIS OF QUANTITY AND ELISABETH VON R.

One year after the publication of the "Preliminary Communication," Freud wrote a paper on the neurotic conditions of which, he believed, he had gained an understanding. He had added obsessional neurosis, and certain other disorders, to hysteria. He entitled this exposition of his view "The Neuro-Psychoses of Defense."[1]

And shortly afterwards, in the chapter on psychotherapy that he contributed to the *Studies,* he wrote, "Strangely enough, I have never in my own experience met with a genuine hypnoid hysteria. Any that I took in hand turned into a defense hysteria."[2] He had concluded that, although some patients did fall into peculiar states that might be designated "hypnoid," the occurrence of such a state was unimportant as an explanatory factor; defense, in his experience, was invariably present, and this could account in every case for the splitting off or unconsciousness of pathogenic ideas.

Freud did not consider his view to be substantially changed. He continued to regard neurosis from the point of view of strangulated affect. He still thought these points central: that the presence of a symptom corresponded to an idea's being unconscious or split off; that a patient suffered from a symptom because an amount of affect belonging to the unconscious idea had not been discharged; and that the symptom would disappear if adequate discharge (abreaction) took place.

1. In the "Neuro-Psychoses of Defense," Freud stated his developed version of the original concept of affective ideas as the "hypothesis of quantity."

> I should like . . . to dwell for a moment on the working hypothesis which I have made use of in this exposition of the neuroses of defense. I refer to the concept that in mental functions something is to be distinguished—a quota of affect or sum of excitation—which possesses all the characteristics of a quantity (though we have no means of measuring it), which is capable of increase, diminution, displacement and discharge, and which is spread over the memory-traces of ideas somewhat as an electrical charge is spread over the surface of a body.
>
> This hypothesis, which, incidentally, already underlies our theory of "abreaction" in our "Preliminary Communication," can be applied in the same sense as physicists apply the hypothesis of a flow of electrical fluid. It is provisionally justified by its utility in coordinating and explaining a great variety of psychical states.[3]

Two uses of the hypothesis may be differentiated. In its first sense (the way in which Freud usually employed it), the quantitative hypothesis may be expanded—in terms of various remarks, conclusions, and applications of it—as follows. The mental unit is an idea (and the paradigm, at least, of an idea is the "memory-trace" of something once perceived or experienced). An affective idea consists of an affective and an ideational component. That is, the idea by itself would be bare, emotionally colorless, and without intensity, but in association with an amount of affect (and/or "psychical excitation") the idea can become a disgusting memory, a strong wish, or a haunting fear.

18

The ideational and affective components are not only conceptually distinguishable, but may in fact be separated from one another and lead separate histories. The usual case is that the affective component is used up, more or less quickly, and the ideational component is worn or fades away in proportion to the loss of its affect. But it can happen that the two components of an affective idea are separated without any decrease of the affect; that they exist within the mind dissociated from one another.

The affect (or excitation, in this sense of the hypothesis sometimes meaning intensity or "impetus") belonging to an idea is a quantity that can be increased or decreased. It is decreased mainly through emotional reactions, and may be increased if, for instance, a situation similar to that which first gave rise to the idea with its associated sum of affect should occur before the original sum of affect is lessened.

A quantity of affect, when separated from one idea, may become attached to another (be displaced onto it). Thus an idea that in its own right would have little intensity, in regard to which the subject would have no strong feeling, may take the place of or be substituted for another, the idea of X, to which affect-excitation had been attached, becoming weak and emotionally colorless, and the substitutive idea of Y becoming intense and associated with strong fear, anger, wishful feeling or impetus, or whatnot.

Two points of the hypothesis of quantity are not directly mentioned in "The Neuro-Psychoses of Defense": that a quantity of affect, when separated from the idea it has been connected with, may, instead of being displaced onto a substitutive idea, undergo "conversion" (e.g., into a "somatic innervation"); and that sums of affect may require discharge when they become excessive; although the subject may choose not to give release to a quantity of affect, as by venting it in action or reaction, it may, therefore, cause an unbearable strain upon him and finally have to seek escape in some—perhaps abnormal—way. Different mental apparatuses have different capacities to withstand such strain.

In its second sense, referring not to "affective ideas" but to their physiological correlates or analogues, the hypothesis is that nervous or neuronic excitation attached to, spread over, or investing a neuron or physical memory-trace (which corresponds to an idea) is capable of increase, decrease, displacement (within the nervous system or on to other memory-traces), and discharge—and may require to be discharged when excessive in amount.

With the use of the hypothesis of quantity Freud extended his original concept of defense into a theory of repression.[4] This theory purported to explain the formation of symptoms in hysteria in terms of strangulation caused by defense, to explain the cure by abreaction, and to correlate these factors; also to explain the existence of unconscious or "split off" ideas, and to correlate the "weakness" or lack of affect, which had earlier been attributed to (most) ideas that could be forgotten, with the formation of symptoms; and at the same time to correlate obsessional neurosis (and, rather more tentatively, certain other mental conditions) with hysteria.

The theory was as follows: an idea arose that was incompatible with a person's ego. Finding the conflict unbearable, the person (or ego) made an effort to get the obnoxious idea out of mind. In consequence, the idea and the affect connected with it were split apart; the idea was "robbed of its affect." Thus a "strong idea" was turned into a "weak one."[5]

What Freud supposed to happen then, in cases of hysteria, he stated thus:

> On this view, the repressed idea would persist as a memory trace that is weak (has little intensity), while the affect that is torn from it would be used for a somatic innervation. (That is, the excitation is "converted.") It would seem, then, that it is precisely through its repression that the idea becomes the cause of morbid symptoms—that is to say, becomes pathogenic.[6]

Repression was thought to work in the same way in cases of obsessional neurosis, except that in these cases, the amount of affect that was removed from an idea by repression was not turned into or used for a somatic innervation, but rather "displaced" onto a substitutive idea.

2. "Strangely enough, I have never in my own experience met with a genuine hypnoid hysteria. Any that *I* took in hand turned into a defense hysteria." It was not, in fact, so very strange that Freud was coming to view defense as a central factor and hypnoid states as comparatively unimportant. He had begun, almost at once, to give up hypnosis as a therapeutic method when he discovered that he was unable to hypnotize many of his patients. Nevertheless, he attempted to help them with "cathartic" therapy. In beginning to make this attempt, Freud had in mind the example of Bernheim's posthypnotic experiments.[7]

When one of Bernheim's subjects was awakened from a hypnotic trance, he would at first be unable to recount what had been said and done during it. But when Bernheim insisted that the subject recall and tell him what had gone on, he would begin to remember—hazily at first, but finally in full and correct detail. It seemed to have been the case that the person was aware, and yet not aware, of what had happened, and that Bernheim's insistence had forced him to become fully aware of what he had ostensibly forgotten.

Freud had from the beginning supposed that a comparable situation existed in cases of neurosis: "the pathogenic groups of ideas . . . were after all certainly present,"[8] but the patient had ostensibly forgotten them.

When Freud and Breuer had hypnotized patients, they asked when the symptoms had developed. If things went as they did in the case of Anna O., the patient told a story that was such that Freud and Breuer could say they had found not only *when* a symptom had developed (following a traumatic event), but also *what* was pathogenic (the memory of the event) and *why* it was pathogenic (because the affect aroused by the event had lacked discharge). Freud now began to work on the hypothesis that using hypnosis was a means that could be dispensed with for eliciting the pathogenic material, which was to be localized in the patient's memories of "traumatic events." A variant of the Bernheim technique could be used as an alternative means to the same end—the recovery of the pathogenic ideas and abreaction.

Armed with his theoretical assumptions and the example of Bernheim, Freud undertook the "cathartic" treatment of Elisabeth von R. (whose case history is the last in the *Studies*) without putting her under hypnosis (because he couldn't). Now he was dealing not with a patient's hypnoid state, but with a patient, Elisabeth. He began by questioning her about her recent life, including the time when her symptoms had become established; she told him a story that was sad enough. She had put all her hopes into her family following her father's death, after having nursed him in his last illness; she had just been feeling that she would like to marry, inspired by the example of her sister's married happiness, when her sister, too, died; now her mother was ill, her brother-in-law estranged from the family, and Elisabeth herself lonely and isolated. But it was nothing that anyone who knew Elisabeth, or the patient herself, could not have reeled straight off, and there was no therapeutic improvement. So Freud assumed that the pathogenic material had not yet been reached; Elisabeth had not told all that she knew, or could be made to know.

Freud now made use of what he called the "pressure technique." He would press his hand on the patient's forehead and ask her to tell him what then occurred to her, whatever it might be. Freud did not try to explain the efficacy of this device in a hypnotist's terms. Instead he said, "I dissociate the patient's attention from his conscious searching and reflecting—from everything, in short, on which he can employ his will—in the same sort of way in which this is effected by staring into a crystal ball, and so on."[9] Under the pressure technique, Elisabeth added to the memories she had already produced, and added some she had not mentioned. One was of having been persuaded to go to a party, while she was nursing

22

her father in his last illness, where she met a man she knew; her happy "erotic" thoughts had suddenly been replaced by self-reproaches when she returned and found her father worse. Freud found that sometimes when he pressed her forehead she would maintain that nothing occurred to her, although there might be a long, preoccupied-seeming pause before she made such a denial, and she *looked* as if she were thinking of something. For these reasons and because of his general assumption that there *must* be something to be recalled in such an illness, Freud decided to work on the hypothesis that there was something that occurred to the patient when she maintained there was not. Elisabeth was holding something back—she was *resisting*.[10] Therefore, he insisted that she tell him everything that occurred to her, and he used his personal influence in various ways to make her do so. And indeed she did then tell him some thought or memory, and sometimes said that she could have told him the first time, but hadn't because she thought it irrelevant or too unpleasant to mention. In this way Freud got Elisabeth to recall some details of the summer before her sister's death, which she had spent at a resort with her mother, sister, and brother-in-law, and when her pains had first become serious.

But Elisabeth was still not well, and during this second period of treatment Freud had begun to have a certain "suspicion" from what Elisabeth had told him of the events. His suspicion was strengthened when the brother-in-law appeared, and Elisabeth was agitated, broke off the session, and was suddenly in pain.

Again Freud renewed his questioning about the events that had taken place at the summer resort. Elisabeth now recalled the events quite fully; for instance, an occasion when her sister, who was ill, had sent her husband off for a long walk with Elisabeth; she had agreed with everything he said—and they discussed all sorts of topics, including intimate ones—and she had wished intensely to have a husband like him. Then, after her sister and brother-in-law had left the place, she had fallen into a reverie on which she imagined what it would be like to be as happy as her sister. On that day her pains had broken out and had remained ever since.

"It had inevitably become clear to me long since what all this was about; but the patient, deep in her bitter-sweet memories, seemed not to notice the end to which she was steering. . . ."[11] Elisabeth went on to tell Freud about her sister's death, which had occurred at the end of that summer. She remembered now that, as she stood at her sister's deathbed, the thought had suddenly occurred to her, "Now he is free again and I can be his wife."[12]

Now Freud put it to Elisabeth that for a long time she had been in love with her brother-in-law. She "made one last desperate effort"[13] to deny it, saying that it *couldn't* be true, she would never forgive herself if she were so wicked. Finally she acknowledged that "what she herself had told me admitted of no other interpretation."[14] After this it required much persuasion—and Freud tried various means—to bring the patient to terms with herself. When they broke off, Elisabeth was much improved.

3. Freud maintained that he had analyzed the case of Elisabeth von R. with the aid of the theory of repression, and cured her through abreaction. His theoretical summary of the case was as follows: Elisabeth's love had, on certain occasions, come into conscious conflict with her ego. She had made an effort of defense against it: the affect-laden idea (or complex) had thus been split into its two components. The quantity of affect connected with the "ideational content" of her love had been cut off from it and employed in forming hysterical symptoms—pains and difficulty in walking—by conversion. The group of ideas that, together with the affect, constituted love, thus became weak and was able to be put aside.

But, although it was the changes in therapeutic practice and observation of cases that are indicated in his report on Elisabeth's case which were leading Freud to expand and adjust his framework of affective ideas, no amount of adjustment and polishing could make the framework gibe with the cases, even if the quantitative conception of affective ideas could be taken as scientific fiction (like or unlike the concept of the fluid electric current). For instance:

A. Unlike distress over the memory of a past event, loving one's brother-in-law doesn't even *seem* like something that could vanish through expression or reaction. A woman might express her love in "verbal" or "motor activity" at every opportunity and to a very great "amount," but one would not expect her thereby to get rid of it.

B. Freud did not try to cure Elisabeth by getting rid of her love in any way. At one point in the treatment, he went out of his way to see whether a marriage might be arranged between Elisabeth and her dead sister's husband—as he put it, to see whether "the girl's wish, of which she was not conscious, (might) come true."[15]

C. Elisabeth did not have pains, as she should have had, instead of or in place of her love. Freud didn't think just that she *had been* in love; what the case centered around was that she *was* in love with her brother-in-law, though she struggled not to recognize it. It was not as if Elisabeth had stopped loving, or as if her love had become weak. Freud may have meant, of course, that the patient's pains replaced her *awareness of* her love. But if the repression theory were to have any explanatory force at all—if it were in any sense to seem that "an idea becomes the cause of morbid symptoms" when and because it is deprived of its affect—then, in the cases to which the theory was applied, it would have to be *as if* the "pathogenic idea" *became weak,* and its affect were employed in forming a symptom.

D. Although Freud said that Elisabeth's symptoms replaced her love, and that the affect torn from her love went to form her pains, on the other hand he asked what had been "turned into physical pain here" and answered that it was "*mental* pain."[16] It would be possible to make out a case for saying that Elisabeth was spared mental pain as long as she remained unconscious of her love—that is, she avoided the extreme distress and conscious self-loathing which the recognition finally cost her. Thus it might seem as if Elisabeth had symptoms in place of distress; the case could be represented by saying it was as if her mental pain had been converted into sensations of physical pain. But the point of the repression theory is to relate the unconsciousness of the "pathogenic idea" (because of the removal of its affect) to the presence of a symptom (because of the conversion or displacement of that same affect). And the conversion of *mental pain* does not explain how *love* of her brother-in-law could remain unconscious.

4. Since this insistence involved effort on my part and so suggested the idea that I had to overcome a resistance, the situation led me at once to the theory that . . . *I had to overcome a psychical force in the patients which was opposed to the pathogenic ideas becoming conscious (being remembered).* A new understanding seemed to open before my eyes when it occurred to me that this must no doubt be the same psychical force which had played a part in the generating of the hysterical symptom. . . .[17]

The hysterical patient's "not knowing" was in fact "not wanting to know". . . .[18]

This girl felt towards her brother-in-law a tenderness whose acceptance into consciousness was resisted by her whole moral being.[19]

Freud had been moving rapidly in two opposite directions at once. While he was expanding the framework of quantity so as to improve its apparent advantage of limiting or reducing the material of observation and of therapeutic practice to the ups and downs of a loaded idea, he was making changes in observation and therapy of such radical scope that the quantity framework could seem to function only by a gross extension of its alternative advantage of looseness and ambiguity.

Freud's discovery of resistance and his equation of it with the "force" of defense was a part of what was leading him to consider something like love to be "pathogenic," rather than the memories of events. Being the same "force," resistance and defense were directed against the same "idea." It had been easy for Elisabeth to recall and tell Freud about the important events in her recent life—so long as in doing so she did not reveal her love for her sister's husband. What she resisted recognizing was precisely her love; Freud thought that what was resisted was what was repressed, what was repressed was what was unconscious, and what was unconscious was pathogenic. What made Freud think that love was the pathogenic idea made him think that the memory of a "traumatic event" was not. Such events, now, could not be considered to have brought about symptoms in the sense that memories of the events were the "immediate causes" of symptoms. But Freud retained part of his concept of a "traumatic event." What he now called "traumatic" was an event (or "moment," or "scene") that provoked an act of defense, thus repression and symptom-formation.

Freud thought that Elisabeth von R. must on certain occasions in the past have become aware of her love for her sister's husband, if only for a moment. He considered that the concept of a defense hysteria required that there be at least one such "traumatic" moment in every case. "Otherwise the conflict that led to the exclusion" from consciousness of Elisabeth's love, for instance, and the consequent formation of her pains, "could not have taken place."[20]

But what Freud proved to Elisabeth in the face of her resistance was that "for a long time (she) had been in love" with her brother-in-law.[21] She had been in love with him, whether or not she knew it. And although Freud could imagine that "defense" was an act—a momentary use of force to press an obnoxious idea out of mind—when he added resistance to defense, it should have become clear that he was talking about a "not wanting to know" which had been in force (as he himself said) for an indefinite period. Elisabeth's love had *always* meant to her being a wicked, hateful person; she had never wanted to be in love, or to recognize that she was. If Elisabeth was unconscious of her love, this meant that she remained unaware of an inclination that, if she had been a different sort of person, she would have recognized for what it was; and she was unaware of what she was doing when she showed her love. In the same sense, she was unconscious of her opposition to her love (her hatred of the "inclination," or of herself for having it). While she remained unaware of her love, she cannot have been aware of hating it; and certainly she did not recognize what she was doing when she resisted becoming aware of it.

Whether or not Elisabeth had ever been conscious of what she opposed in herself, her being unconscious of it was not the result of having been conscious of it at some time, nor of having directed some psychical force against it, nor of having performed an *act* of defense against it. It was rather the case that because Elisabeth's love was in conflict with her "whole moral being"—because of what it meant to her—she had not faced her love nor recognized her hatred of herself for loving. She was in a state of conflict, and was unconscious that she was.

But then the events that Freud induced Elisabeth to recall were not "traumatic" even in the watered-down sense that he tried to maintain. They had not brought it about that her love was repressed. In fact, Freud made it clear that he assumed Elisabeth must at some time have been conscious of her love only to meet the requirements of his theory. He gave as an example of a probable such event Elisabeth's having thought at her sister's deathbed that her brother-in-law was now free and could marry her. But during the treatment Elisabeth recalled the "scene," and the thought that had then occurred to her, without recognizing, even then, that she was and had been in love with the man. If this implies that Elisabeth was quite abnormally blind to certain emotions of her own, that is part of what Freud was getting at when he said that her love was unconscious and that she resisted becoming aware of it. What Freud reported of the case makes it seem highly unlikely that Elisabeth had ever become fully aware of her love before Freud made her recognize it. The most important events that Elisabeth recalled seem to have been simply occasions when, as Freud said, her love (and her pains) were at their height: he might have said that they were occasions when her unconscious conflict was at its height. They did not cause her symptoms even in the sense that they caused her to be unaware of her love (nor did they cause her love, nor her opposition to her love, unless love in general is caused by experiences of being with a lovable person).

If the patient's love was not forced into unconsciousness at some moment by an act or the employment of some force, then defense could be distinguished from resistance only on rather arbitrary and trivial grounds: defense was the patient's opposition to some love or hate, wish or fear of his own, manifested in his unawareness when he would first, if he had not opposed it, have recognized it; resistance was the same opposition manifested later, in therapeutic recalcitrance.

Furthermore, if the patient was unconscious of his opposition in the same sense that he was unconscious of what he opposed (and if the appearance of symptoms could not be attributed to his having at that time driven what he opposed out of consciousness) then what had made Freud think that the "idea" the patient opposed was in itself pathogenic (his equation of that which could be supposed to be put down by the ego's defense with the resisted-repressed-unconscious-pathogenic) could no longer carry weight.[22]

In spite of all this, Freud's assumption that pathogenic material was to be localized in points of time—these points being the events following which, or upon which, the patient's symptoms had been established, or had become severe—was, up to a point, useful. By his close questioning of Elisabeth on the details of such events, he did discover something that was unconscious and that appeared to be troubling the patient: not memories of events as such, but Elisabeth's love, and what it meant to her. For the therapist, the patient's love and her opposition to it were the inevitable interpretation of her recital of the memories. The memories were important as a text in which to discover the problem. The conflict could be localized in the events in the sense that the memories revealed the conflict, and also in the sense that they allowed Freud to pin it down—this opposed and that opposing. If he had *begun* by looking for something as diffuse and elusive as a love of which the patient was unaware, and a hatred of this love, he might have had a hard time finding it. And if he had looked for what was in fact even more diffuse than this statement of the conflict would indicate (Elisabeth's opposition could be variously defined as her not wanting to know, her reasons for not wanting to know, what her love meant to her, her belief that loving this man was wicked—her whole moral being) he might have found even more difficulty getting a grip on it. For the patient, the memories were important as a text that she, having provided it, could not deny, and that, she had to admit, did lead inevitably to the conclusion Freud drew. They were the means of making her aware of her conflict with herself.

> 5. Nor does the treatment consist of extirpating anything—psychoanalysis is not able to do this for the present—but in causing the resistance to melt and in thus enabling the circulation to make its way into a region that has hitherto been cut off.[23]

> The patient only gets free from the hysterical symptom by reproducing the pathogenic impressions that caused it, and by giving utterance to them with an expression of affect, and thus the therapeutic task *consists solely of inducing him to do so.* . . . [emphasis in original][24]

Because Freud discovered resistance by looking for a pathogenic idea and undertook the task of "melting resistance" as an alternative to using hypnosis, and because he had all along considered that it was solely the abreaction of the affect belonging to the pathogenic idea which could affect a cure, it is understandable that he conceived of resistance, theoretically, merely as a force blocking the way to the pathogenic material—as if it were to be dealt with only before what the patient opposed in himself was made conscious, and only in order to make it conscious.

Yet Freud adapted his practice to the exigencies of a therapeutic situation in which it became evident that a neurotic's resistance was an opposition that had been in force before the beginning of his treatment; it was not *a* force, and it did not vanish when the patient became more aware of what he opposed in himself. What did happen, when Freud confronted Elisabeth with her love, was that "the recovery of this repressed idea had a shattering effect on the poor girl. She cried aloud when I put the situation drily before her. . . ."25 And when Elisabeth had to acknowledge the correctness of his interpretation, she was for a time in worse condition than before. She had kept herself unaware of her love because loving this man meant to her being a wicked, hateful person; now she thought that she was wicked, and consciously hated herself. (Nor did her pains disappear at once.)

Freud did not—as his official theory of abreaction would seem to have required—leave Elisabeth in such a condition. And although (usually) he limited the term "resistance" to the patient's opposition as manifested in therapy, before what was opposed became conscious, what he did when he said he was "melting resistance" was by no means limited to clearing the way to the "ideas" that he labeled "pathogenic." Freud mentions some of the measures that he included under the general title of "melting resistance" in the following passage:

> What means have we at our disposal for overcoming this continual resistance? In the first place, we must reflect that a psychical resistance, especially one that has been in force for a long time, can only be resolved slowly, and by degrees. . . . But lastly—and this remains the strongest lever—we must endeavor, after we have discovered the motives for his resistance, to deprive them of their value or even to replace them by more powerful ones. This no doubt is where it ceases to be possible to state psychotherapeutic activity in formulas. One works to the best of

one's power, as an elucidator (where ignorance has given rise to fear), as a teacher, as the representative of a freer and superior view of the world, as a father confessor who gives absolution, as it were, by a continuance of his sympathy and respect after the confession has been made.[26]

What was Freud doing, then, when he melted resistance? He had to find out why as well as what was opposed; one could become fully clear only when the other was clear. And, although all the processes—of discovering an opposed inclination or motive, of finding out the "motives for resistance," of modifying or melting the resistance—were gradual, so that one could hardly say which came first, the bringing of unconscious conflict into the open could almost be said to have been the beginning of what Freud did to help a patient. He was concerned to modify or replace the motives for resistance, and if he succeeded in doing this, he was doing something more than making the patient aware of what he opposed in himself and why he opposed it.

Freud said this was the point at which it ceased to be possible to state psychotherapeutic activities in formulas. He was right, of course; what Freud did in any particular case depended on why *this* patient was opposed to some love, hate, wish, or whatnot of his own. But what Freud accomplished by the various measures he took might be summed up in a general formula: He helped the patient stop being opposed, or merely opposed—and this is the same as saying that he helped the patient to resolve a conflict, or at least to reduce it to manageable proportions. The patient might be right to think that he ought not, for instance, to gratify some wish or hate; Freud thus, in one sense, would not want him to stop being opposed to it. But Freud, perhaps acting as a "father confessor," could help him accept his possession of such feelings, and believe that he was nevertheless a worthwhile person—in short, stop simply fighting with himself and begin to find a *modus vivendi*.

Other therapeutic measures that Freud undertook, which he did not refer to as "melting resistance," similarly had the tendency of helping the patient to become reconciled with himself. An instance is his matchmaking in the case of Elisabeth von R. Elisabeth thought loving her brother-in-law was despicable, and an offense to her beloved family; a way to convince her that she did not have to take it that way was to show her that Freud (the "representative of a freer and superior view of the world") considered it something that could be justified in sight of God and man. (Also, no doubt, he hoped to find for her an arrangement whereby she could love, without having any reason to hate herself for loving. He referred to the possibility of a marriage as "the *solution* for which Elisabeth longed.")[27]

What Freud *did*, therefore, which was intended to, and which apparently sometimes did, have the effect of helping a patient, was to make him aware of a conflict of which he had been unconscious, and to make progress, at least, toward its resolution. And this was *all* that he did, but Freud continued to think he was doing something else. He continued to think that although he "extirpated" nothing (and never tried to get rid of, for instance, Elisabeth's "pathogenic" love), she was cured, if at all, through "abreaction."

"Abreaction" had clearly lost the sense in which it held together the strangulation view, but there was just enough resemblance in the way Freud now treated patients to what he had previously given that title so that he could retain the term and hold that patients were cured by recalling and uttering their memories of "traumatic events" with an expression of affect—and even that what brought about improvement was the patient's being relieved of affect.

What function the patient's recollections of events had in Freud's therapy, I have already suggested. The memories were the means by which the patient became aware of an inner conflict. They allowed Freud, and through him the patient, to pin down the conflict and to come to grips with it. The patient's utterance of the memories in itself relieved him of neither symptoms nor his intolerable mental condition. Nor did the patient's utterance of his opposition have such an effect (nor—

what was the same thing—his expression of an "affect" in regard to what he opposed). But, as Freud said of a woman patient, "She had to overcome the distressing effect aroused by having been able to entertain such a wish. . . ."[28] That is, the patient not only had to become aware of her wish and what it meant to her—to recognize that she had the wish and was distressed by it—but she also had to overcome her distress: in other words, come to accept her wish (not necessarily being willing to gratify it, but not being horrified by it as before). What Freud referred to as a period of "abreaction" in the case of Elisabeth von R. was a period in which the patient discussed in detail her feelings, how they had developed, what she thought of them—and what to do with them. Gradually she became more able to come to terms with her love for her sister's husband. In one sense, she not only expressed, but was relieved of—or, better, overcame—an "affect": that is, her blind loathing of herself for loving the man. But although Freud singled out such phases of therapy as periods of "abreaction," if the term meant that the patient recalled events or became aware of emotions and overcame an "affect," then "abreaction" was going on throughout the treatment, as was "melting resistance." There could be no distinction between the two.

6. Freud's history of the case of Elisabeth von R. suggests that he began the case with a series of assumptions, and a therapeutic technique, that were in accordance with the quantitative theory—but ended it with a set of assumptions or implicit hypotheses, and a method of treatment, that were in accord with quite a different theory, centering on the concept of unconscious conflict, or the concept of emotions that cannot be acknowledged because of what they mean to the subject. Various observations in other papers are in accord with the implicit theory of unconscious conflict rather than with the official theory of quantity.

I speak of an implicit theory, rather than of the beginning of a therapeutic technique and a number of disparate observations, because the concept of conflict can be seen as the center of a theory that, though still in many respects incomplete, was coherent in itself as well as being in accord with the material of observation as Freud reported it; and also because, as I shall show later, Freud continued to treat neurotics as if he held such a theory, gained material to fill in the original outline, and attempted, later on, to incorporate some of the material that I would attribute to the implicit theory into his official formulations.

Stated most briefly, the implicit theory, in its primitive form, is as follows: Neurotics suffer primarily from severe emotional conflicts of which they are unconscious. Such a conflict is at the center of a neurotic's disturbed mental condition, and his or her neurotic symptoms issue from it. The general condition can be improved, and symptoms alleviated, if progress can be made toward the resolution of the conflict, and to help the patient resolve an unconscious conflict is the therapist's primary endeavor; making the conflict conscious is part of the attempt to help the patient come to terms with himself.

A. Unconscious Conflict

The examples reported by Freud indicate that the type of emotional conflict that is in question may be provisionally defined as a mental condition in which a person opposes, tries to ignore, or tries to rid himself of (and tries not to act upon) a strong tendency, emotion, or inclination of his own, as of love or hate for another person.

That such a conflict exists is the therapist's interpretation of the patient's conduct, as observed in the course of treatment and as reported by the patient, and of the memories that he dwells upon when pressed to remember past events in detail. The patient's opposition becomes evident especially in his reluctance to recall details of certain events and to interpret his conduct and memories as revealing the inclination that the therapist sees in them. Hypothetically, too, he may at some point voice a fear or loathing of the inclination posited: e.g.,

"If that were true I should hate myself," or, "That can't be true, I'm not so wicked." To say that the conflict is unconscious is to say that the patient does not interpret his conduct and memories as indicative of it; he is not aware of what he is doing when he shows his inclination or his opposition to it.

The phenomena of resistance—including such remarks as "That can't be true, I can't be that wicked"—suggest that the patient *has not become aware of the tendency in himself that he hates or fears because he does not want to be aware of it, i.e., precisely because he does hate or fear it.*

It is a question in what sense a neurotic is unaware or unconscious of an inner conflict. In some sense he must be always aware of an inclination, if he opposes it. Freud's examples suggest that there are, so to speak, levels or degrees of awareness.[29] The case of Elisabeth von R. is interesting in this respect.

When Freud first confronted Elisabeth with his interpretation of her memories—that she had for a long time been in love with her brother-in-law—she expressly refused to believe that she was capable of such wickedness. However, she did not reject the possibility cooly; she "cried aloud," and was "shattered" at the thought. It would seem, then, that although she was now "aware" of a conflict in herself in a new sense, in another sense she remained "unaware" of it. She was aware that Freud interpreted what she had told him as indicative of the conflict, but in the sense that she refused to believe him right, she remained unaware that she loved the man; as Freud remarked, she was still trying desperately not to have to face her love of him.

Even when Elisabeth had to acknowledge that Freud's interpretation was correct, it could be argued that she was not fully aware of her inner conflict: acknowledging that an argument about oneself must be or seems to be correct is not necessarily the same as feeling or altogether believing it to be true. Elisabeth was in the position of one who says "It must be so," yet still did not see herself as the person who loved her brother-in-law.

This line of thought leads to the conclusion that Elisabeth became fully conscious of her love for her brother-in-law only when she was able to feel and believe that she could love the man.[30] But Freud's report suggests that she could do this only when she ceased attempting to repudiate or fend off the inclination. (As long as she said to herself "I cannot be so wicked," she could not feel that she did love the man.) Thus Freud's dictum that the patient's "not knowing" *is* "not wanting to know" seems to take on a fuller meaning than he recognized. Elisabeth did not stop trying to repudiate or fend off her love for the man until her conviction that it was wicked and hateful was lessened. It would seem, then, that her becoming fully conscious of the inclination she was fending off coincided with a mitigation of the conflict between that inclination and her belief that it was monstrous.

B. Conflict and Symptoms

According to the implicit theory of this period, neurotic symptoms begin or are aggravated at times when the unconscious conflict is at its height. They issue, somehow, from the conflict. Freud was working on the supposition that symptoms "take the place of" the repressed idea or affect, or of something like mental pain. Two kinds of comments of his suggest alternative interpretations of this hypothesis that could form part of the implicit theory.

On the one hand, his comment that a patient like Elisabeth von R. felt pains in her legs instead of mental pain could be taken in the sense that her hysterical symptoms were not so much an expression as a misinterpretation of emotion.

On the other hand, Freud said that Elisabeth "spared herself the painful conviction" that she was in love by "inducing physical pains in herself instead."[31] This suggests that he was thinking of the symptoms as brought about by a purpose of the patient's—the purpose, that is, of fending off, remaining in ignorance of, or distracting herself from her love, because it meant to her being hateful and wicked. At the end of the chapter on psychotherapy Freud defined certain "transference wishes" as new neurotic symptoms precisely because they seemed to be products of resistance. It is because he could say this sort of thing while at the same time promulgating the quantitative theory of repression and symptom-formation that I speak of an implicit theory.

The "spared herself the painful conviction" formula is suggestive not just of considering a neurotic symptom as the patient's way of distracting herself from a conflict. If we suppose that Elisabeth gave herself symptoms in an attempt to keep herself unaware of her love, because she hated herself for having it, we may ask why did she try to spare herself pain by giving herself *pains?* The "mental pain" that Elisabeth spared herself was the conscious conviction that she was a hateful person for loving her sister's husband: it was conscious self-loathing. Her self-loathing did not go out of existence when it was unconscious. Might the supposition that Elisabeth "induced pains in herself" in an attempt to keep herself unaware of her love, because she hated herself for it, be in part reformulated: Elisabeth gave herself pains because she hated herself for loving the man? If so, then the hysterical symptoms in this case might be seen as a form of self-punishment as well as a form of self-distraction. On the other hand, the sensations Elisabeth had were not *simply* painful, as Freud noted when he examined the affected areas and the patient assumed an expression as of sensual ecstasy.

(Note: The ups and downs of Elisabeth's symptoms tended to support the theory that she gave them to herself in an effort to remain unconscious of her love, or to punish herself for it. The pain was intense when Freud first told the girl of his interpretation. At that point she was not conscious that he was right; she was desperately holding to a conscious belief that she did not love the man. The symptoms did not greatly abate until the end of the treatment; at that time she was not so inclined to believe that loving her brother-in-law was hateful and wicked.)

C. Material for Expansion of the Concept of Conflict

The cases with which Freud was now dealing were presenting him already with material to expand the view that I have just outlined. Freud used a patient's memories of events that had taken place at about the time when his symptoms were established to define, and to demonstrate to the patient, a conflict he had with himself. But he was gaining material that could show not only that the conflict defined by these events was not something that *occurred* at these moments—that it was in force until he helped the patient to resolve it—but also that it might have a broader scope than he at first believed.

Freud was beginning to notice a phenomenon that he called "transference." In the "Psychotherapy" he gave an example: A (typical) woman patient who, having made herself unaware, because it horrified her, of an old wish that some man would make love to her, found herself in the course of therapy wishing that Freud would kiss her, and was horrified at herself for entertaining such a wish for an instant. The conflict had come up in a new form, in new circumstances. In such a case, Freud might have said that the patient was in a conflict with herself between prudishness and erotic feelings or desires in general. But he preferred to put it that the wish in regard to Freud was a substitute for the wish that was unconscious: it was at the same time an indication of the unconscious wish and a cover for it. Freud preferred to speak of the present wish as a substitute for the unconscious one because he had reason to believe that it was artificial: the patient would never have had it if she had not had the unconscious wish, and if it had not been that the course of the treatment was leading her to discover the wish in its "historical instance." What horrified her was not so much the new wish in itself as the new wish because it was a cover for the old one. Freud thought that to the patient the present wish was in more than one respect a way of keeping herself unaware of its prototype: her horror over it distracted her from the original desire and disrupted the treatment, which was leading to its discovery. Having such a "symptom" was a form of resistance.

And, Freud was finding material that might have led him (and of a sort that later did lead him) to view the central conflict in a case of neurosis as having a longer history than he at first supposed.

For instance, in the case history of Elisabeth von R., Freud noted that the patient's hysterical pains had not made their first appearance at the time of the "traumatic events" concerning the brother-in-law. She had been slightly troubled by them when she was nursing her father in his last illness. Freud found in Elisabeth's memories a "scene" that he thought might account for a "preliminary conversion"—the occasion when Elisabeth had been persuaded to leave her nursing for an evening and had returned full of "blissful" thoughts about the young man who saw her home, only to "repress her erotic idea from consciousness" "under the pressure of lively self-reproaches"[32] when she found her dying father worse.

But the pains had not appeared at precisely that moment. Freud was therefore inclined to think that when they first appeared they were not hysterical, but rheumatic or "spinal-neurasthenic." He wanted, however, to retain the "scene" as "traumatic": the move he made was to hypothesize (as he had done in other cases) that when the hysterical symptoms were established, it was because of a "summation of traumas." This hypothesis seemed to fit the quantitative theory: in Elisabeth's case, it was only when the affect split away from the repressed erotic idea concerning the first man was joined by a further amount of detached affect from a similar idea that it became the cause of symptoms. It was a "question of how much affective tension . . . an organism can tolerate."[33]

In the midst of his attempts to estimate amounts of affective tension, Freud noted that at this "traumatic moment" Elisabeth had been involved in a conflict "exactly similar" to that which later appeared as the center of her neurosis. He meant that then, as later, Elisabeth's moral standards and conception of her duties, in particular to her family, came into conflict with an erotic "idea."

He did not, however, pay attention to an odd point of similarity between the first occasion and something that happened later; that is, the thought that occurred to Elisabeth at her sister's deathbed. It would seem possible to say that on this later occasion Elisabeth, though grieved at her sister's death, was glad of it in that it meant that her brother-in-law was free for herself. It seems peculiar that the same girl had previously reproached herself bitterly for indulging in the pleasure of mild courtship because when she was indulging in it her dying father became worse—as if she thought it was her fault that he became worse.

If Freud had gone more deeply into this peculiarity of the case (and into the "summation of traumas" in other cases) it might have begun to seem that what Elisabeth—for instance—rejected so vehemently in herself was not just her love for a particular man; or, to put it another way, that her reasons for rejecting her love for her brother-in-law as violently as she did were not so obvious as Freud thought; or again, that there were not two separate, though similar conflicts in the case, but that Elisabeth's struggle with herself was wider in scope than Freud, at this point, considered it to be. The similarity between the two situations or instances of conflict does not explain the violence of Elisabeth's opposition, but it suggests that in some form her conflict may have been present even before the episode of the first young man. Why should she have felt as she did in either instance?

7. A remarkable but not a surprising characteristic of Freud's early invocations of the central nervous system (there are no later ones) is that there is very little neurology in them. The *Project for a Scientific Psychology* (1895) was, mainly, as Freud made clear in his introductory remarks, an attempt to map out, on a semi-imaginary locale, what is involved in neurotic symptoms and a variety of other "mental processes," from the point of view of the hypothesis of quantity. Freud meant to work with a few hypotheses; the preliminary assumptions were that the brain unit (corresponding to an idea) was the neuron, and that nervous or neuronic excitation (corresponding, up to a

point, with affect or "psychical excitation") consisted of "quantities in a condition of flow," investing or occupying neurons, and subject to processes of increase, displacement, and so on. Freud stated that his particular concept of neuronic excitation was based on "processes" (involving affect of "psychical excitation") "that had to be described" in cases of neurosis.[34]

One evident difficulty on which the *Project* ran aground (it was abandoned and not published until 1950) was the strange character of the "explanation" that was being offered: on the one hand, it was an attempted translation of the "mental" factors (affective ideas and the "processes" to which they were supposed to be subject) into fictional correlates, in order, as Freud said, to make the "processes which had to be described" "perspicuous and free from contradictions,"[35] and on the other hand the explanation was in terms of entities and processes behind the "psychical" ones, which had to be taken as literally, or hypothetically, going on in another sphere or arena. It was not only that, given this locale, the explanation being given seemed, though partly such as might be afforded by a model, also partly such as might be afforded by postulates as to the actual workings of the central nervous system, but also that some of the vicissitudes ascribed to neuronic excitation were not related to the "processes that had to be described" in the same way that the preliminary postulates were. (An amount of excitation, because it is excessive and at the same time denied discharge by its normal paths, has overcome "resistances" or "contact-barriers" and is, say, stimulating a visual center and thus producing a hallucination.) Freud was switching between trying to give an explanation in terms of a translation-fiction and one in terms of postulated background occurrences— which, however, were based on the translation.

But replacing "processes" of displacement of affect with processes of flux of neuronic excitation does not magically produce a neurological explanation, even if it takes into consideration some facts or conjectures concerning cerebral anatomy; and a "process" of displacement of affect is not itself clarified by replacing it with its neurological shadow.

Aside from the nonexplanation offered by the replacement of "psychical" processes with processes affecting particles and quantities in the nervous system, the nervous system counters, however shadowlike, could not perform the functions of an "affective idea." Freud's intention to proceed with a few simple hypotheses was soon defeated. Almost at once, for instance, he found it necessary to postulate the existence of three different systems of neurons. Each problem of translation from "affective ideas" and the processes to which affect was assumed to be subject into the neurological picture led to at least one hypothesis, assumption, or "construction"; each gap or incongruity within the schema was stopped up with another hypothesis, and each hypothesis led only to further postulates—and with the proliferation of hypotheses, assumptions, and constructions, nothing was perspicuous and devoid of contradictions. This proliferation may be partly accountable in terms of the peculiar status of the particles and quantities in question: they could move according to their own logic, and indeed could make up their own rules as they went along. But a central reason for the gaps and the ensuing ad hoc solutions was the narrowness of the framework: the counters were too few; everything had to be accounted for in terms of excitation and its limited vicissitudes.

The irony of the matter was that Freud attributed the failure of the *Project* to the impossibility (in the contemporary state of knowledge) of making the second step of translation: that is, locating mental processes in the brain, and identifying "ideas" with neurons and amounts of "psychical excitation" with quantities of neuronic excitation. Freud remarked in 1915, in the metapsychological paper on "The Unconscious," that "every attempt" to make such a translation "has miscarried completely."[36] Yet in the direction of the development of the hypothesis of quantity as dealing with ideas and affect, Freud was taking a fatal first step of translation—translating the case material he covered with the terminology of "affective ideas" into affective ideas—and later works, notably the metapsychological papers, "miscarried" in much the same manner as the *Project*.

Again, it was a strange kind of explanation that was being offered. Freud certainly recognized, at least from time to time, that his use of the affective ideas/quantity terminology in application to specific cases was different from his use of it in theoretical formulations. He thought, correctly, that his use of the language in specific cases was loose; apparently he thought, incorrectly, that his theoretical formulations were just tightening and clarifying what he had to deal with: abstracting the factors that were central for explanation and correlation of the data, and excluding peripheral considerations. On the one hand, Freud's psychical-quantity theories seemed to be providing an explanation in terms of these same "affective ideas" (later, "infantile wishes," "component impulses") that he encountered in his cases, and the vicissitudes or processes in question were supposed to be theirs; on the other hand, the theories seemed to be explaining the data in terms of entities and processes to be taken, literally or hypothetically, as existing and going on behind the "unconscious love" or emotional conflict with which he was dealing in practice. The arena was a semi-fictional "mental apparatus" or "psyche"—a sort of limbo.

But what Freud was dealing with from the outset in particular cases was a person's emotions, beliefs, and desires, and his or her "not wanting to know"—not the distribution or elimination of sums of affect or excitation. The affective ideas/quantity framework was a fiction, but it was not a scientific fiction. It did not provide valuable hypotheses about what might lie behind neurotic phenomena, nor a model, nor a metaphorical account of the material and what could explain it, nor a clarification of what was involved in the cases. It was the material covered by "affective ideas," and not affective ideas, that was providing the ingredients of an explanation. Just this material was excluded when the terms that loosely covered it were tightened again; there was, for example, no counter or move corresponding to wanting not to know that one is in love because it would mean being a wicked person.

Freud's theoretical tightening not only was eliminating just the material that did provide the basis for an explanation, but was also erecting a facade that covered and hid the nature of the case material and of Freud's interpretations.

Consider the following sequence. When Freud tried to translate Elisabeth von R.'s unconscious love into repressed ideational content plus converted quantity of affect/energy, he was led to remark, in the case history, that it is inaccurate to speak of "unconscious love," because an affective idea or complex, in being repressed, is reduced to an ideational content—a bare, weak notion, its affect torn away and employed in conversion or displacement. Thus, there could be no unconscious love as such, and no unconscious fears or wishes, only their disintegrated remains.[37] In translating what he was finding to be a central factor in a neurosis—an "unconscious" love, hate, etc.—into an affective idea, so as to explain its repression, Freud explained it right away.

But then he had to replace or reinstate it, with further hypotheses concerning not emotions or beliefs but affective ideas. From within Freud's framework, there did not seem to be a problem with the quantity theory of repression, but a problem to be solved. That is, if an idea such as Elisabeth's love has been deprived of its affect or excitation, thereby becoming weak and able to be put out of mind (or, rather, put down into a layer of the mind from which it cannot escape), why does it afterwards present itself as such a strong, seemingly *affective* idea? Why does the patient have to expend so much energy in keeping it down, if it has lost its force?

In 1915, when Freud wrote the paper on "The Unconscious," he had given up the idea that the formation of neurotic symptoms corresponded with repression (as they might appear long after repression was assumed to have occurred) and he had, on the whole, substituted "psychical excitation" or "libido" for the affective component, but his theory that repression consists of the disintegration of an affective (or energy-laden) idea remained. He encountered the difficulty that was just mentioned, and he tried to meet it with a further hypothesis concerning repression.

He asked how it can be that a repressed idea, which must be

assumed to have been deprived of its preconscious cathexis—that is, its investment with excitation in or of the "dominant system" of the mind—can remain strong, or "capable of action," as unconscious wishes may be. He answered that the idea must be supposed to have retained an *un*conscious cathexis, or to have received fresh energy from the mobile store of excitation assumed to exist in the unconscious. This hypothesis, however, was met by a further problem: how such a therefore strong, affect- or energy-laden idea could remain unconscious, rather than repeatedly breaking through into consciousness and having to be shorn again and again of its excitation. Freud plugged up the problems with his further hypothesis that the preconscious system (System Pcs.) sets up "anticathexes" to block the emergence of such ideas into consciousness.[38]

Freud's continual system-building that answered to the exigencies of the idea/quantity framework, his partial distortion and partial removal from consideration and covering-over of those factors that could have yielded an explanation relevant to the cases, were not limited to an isolable portion of his work. These confusions were more prominent in certain works and in certain aspects of the field of inquiry—for instance, in the seventh chapter of *The Interpretation of Dreams* as against chapters II through V,[39] in the metapsychological and other "technical" papers as against case histories, and concerning the causes or genesis of neurosis, and the genesis or production of dreams, as against the "interpretation of dreams" and the analysis of symptoms. But I will show that apparently quantity-free formulations were leaning on a model contained in the quantity theory, and that what I call the wish-fulfillment-mind direction was ultimately more responsive to the ex-quantity model than to the data. Nevertheless, no formulation, however evidently responsive to the idea/quantity framework as against the character of the material, ought to be set aside as altogether irrelevant.

Each development of the quantity direction was a compromise, as between a previous theory (not necessarily the last enunciated) and the data of observation, or between previous theories, and within each of these developments the underlying problems (and assets) of the dual capacity of Freud's language to operate loosely and tightly was at work. These facts account for defects in these theories additional to the strange kind of "explanation" they provide and their substantial irrelevance to and putting out of consideration of the implicit account, and at the same time for the impossibility of discarding altogether everything that is stated in quantity terms and contexts.

One of the defects in all the developments of the quantity theory is the inclusion in them, as central concepts, of incomplete fusions of different concepts. The original concept of "affect" was an attempt to fuse emotion and excitation (energy or force). Freud's "affect" was not much either of emotion or excitation, and it was not much of a fusion. The central concept was irresolvably ambiguous, hovering between the ingredient concepts, and in using it Freud sometimes hovered and sometimes vacillated between the ingredients. The concept of "affective ideas," which, with its descendants, was central in all the quantity developments, depended on the fusion-concept of affect; in using the term, Freud vacillated between using it merely as a name first for something like a fearful memory, later for an inclination, emotion, desire, or whatever, and using it with the implication that the "affective idea" was an ideational content, or memory-trace, plus affect or excitation.

The "infantile wishes" of the theory of primary and secondary processes were an attempted fusion of wishes with "affective ideas" (memory-trace and cathexis). "Wish-fulfillment" in this theory was an attempted fusion of satisfaction, gratification, or fulfillment of desires with reduction in level of endopsychic excitation; the attempted fusion included a third element, to hold the first two together: pleasure, or relief from unpleasure (the feeling-state corresponding to reduction of excess excitation, and, as influx of excitation from a somatic need could only be stopped by fulfillment or satisfaction of the need, corresponding to gratification). Again, the fusions were unsatisfactory in themselves. Sometimes considering "wish-fulfillment" as reduction of excitation, sometimes as satisfaction of a desire (or need), Freud's concept of satisfaction remained tinged with the concept of relief from excess excitation. (One of the secondary results of this tinging was a blurring of the distinction between expression and satisfaction.)

The tendency of all the developments of the quantity theory[40] to split in two—so that there is a hard-quantity version and a semiquantitative version, on the one hand closely bound to the quantity-level, and on the other hand mediating, more or less, between it and the material—is related to the basis of the quantity theories in attempted fusions. For example, the mediating theory of what I call wish-fulfillment-mind splits off from the processes theory by dropping the excitation and discharge as such, and carrying on the wishes and fulfillment, heavily tinged with the excitation model. The existence of closely related but irreconcilable variants and the lack of clear differentiation among the variants allows semiexternal level-switching, shifting, shuffling, and borrowing in any given passage, and often from one sentence to the next.

The virtue of these defects is that, although every part and level of the explicit theory is infected with the irrelevant questions and answers (and the models) generated by the quantity framework, few parts and no level as a whole are altogether without relevance to the material.

Here is an example, again from the metapsychological papers. Freud is asking himself whether it would be preferable to adopt the hypothesis that a change "from Ucs. to Cs. (or Pcs.) . . . involves a fresh record . . . of the idea in question, which may thus be situated as well in a fresh psychical locality" or to postulate "that the transposition consists in a change in the state of the idea, a change involving the same material and occurring in the same locality?" He introduces as supporting the fresh-registration hypothesis "observations from psychoanalytic practice," to wit that "If we communicate to a patient some idea which he has at one time repressed but which we have discovered in him, our telling him makes at first no change in his mental condition. . . . At this point, . . . the pa-

48

tient has in actual fact the same idea in two forms in two separate localities of his metal apparatus. . . . Now in reality there is no lifting of the repression until the conscious idea . . . has united with the unconscious memory-trace. Only through bringing the latter itself into consciousness is the effect achieved." But then he decides that this consideration does not really settle the question because "to have heard something and to have experienced something are in their psychological nature two quite different things, even though the content of both is the same." He shelves the choice between the two hypotheses.[41]

The passage, I think, is to be diagnosed as involving not only a general confusion as to level (or what the theory is about) and a palpable shift from the metapsychological or idea-quantitative (in which an idea is a thing, to be unconscious of which is to contain it somewhere in oneself below the barriers) to the psychological ("to have heard something," etc.) and back; but also the lifting of a practical consideration (that to be told one entertains such and such an "idea," or even to admit that one's possession of it is the inescapable interpretation of a tale one has been telling, is not necessarily to be fully aware that it is one's own) from the level on which it belongs, its investiture in disfiguring terms (at first there are two ideas of the same content present in the mental apparatus: one must perceive the very idea that has been repressed), and its presentation as if it were only spun out to fill an unnecessary gap in an irrelevant theory.

Even the hypotheses of withdrawal of preconscious cathexis, retention of unconscious excitation, and anticathexis, which I mentioned earlier as exemplifying the self-begotten proliferation of the quantity system, are not only that; at least, it is easy to see that a practicing analyst might maintain the first postulate on the ground that his patients were not fully aware of their "unconscious ideas" and were in one sense ignoring them, the second on the ground that the "ideas" in question were nonetheless operative, expressible, and central to the subjects, and the third on the ground that the patients demonstrated great "resistance" or "not wanting to know." But if he thought of these factors of observation as evidence for something beyond themselves, properly stated as the theoretical hypotheses, he would be mistaken; and if he vacillated between thinking "anticathexis" the same as "not wanting to know" and thinking it something beyond that, in another sphere, he would be confused.

3. WISH-FULFILLMENT-QUANTITY WISH-FULFILLMENT-MIND

If a hysteric is surprised at having to be so frightened of something trivial or if a man suffering from obsessions is surprised at such distressing self-reproaches arising out of a mere nothing, they have both gone astray, because they regard the ideational content—the triviality or the mere nothing—as what is essential: and they put up an unsuccessful fight because they take this ideational content as the starting point of their thought-activity. Psycho-analysis can put them upon the right path by recognizing the affect as being, on the contrary, justified and by seeking out the idea which belongs to it but has been repressed and replaced by a substitute.[1]

In the short time between the publication of the *Studies* and that of *The Interpretation of Dreams,* there was a notable change in Freud's method of clinical investigation: he came to use the technique of "free association" for interpreting neurotic symptoms, dreams, and other phenomena. Partly through the application of the new method of investigation, the material Freud had to deal with was greatly enlarged, and some important new discoveries were made. Partly to accommodate some of the new findings, there was an apparently substantial shift in the central concepts of Freud's explicit theory, and the theory was expanded to cover a wider field of inquiry and to cover it in more detail than previous theories could afford. The explicit theory of Freud's maturity, introduced in *The Interpretation of Dreams,* is far more complex, and unwieldy to discuss, than the theories that preceded it. At the same time, as I mentioned in Chapter II, the explicit theory split into two distinguishable levels or directions. And, I shall argue, the implicit theory of unconscious conflict was further developed at the same time.

In one direction, Freud continued in the line of his previous theory of repression by the splitting apart of affective ideas and symptom-formation by conversion or displacement of their detached quantitative components. Taking into prime account two of his recent discoveries, formulated as the findings that the "pathogenic material" is "infantile,"[2] and that a hysterical attack, for instance, is not merely a "discharge" but an "action,"[3] or that neurotic symptoms and dreams are "wish-fulfillments,"[4] the theory of primary and secondary processes, presented in the seventh chapter of *The Interpretation of Dreams,* brings these findings together with a view that a dream or neurotic symptom is the outcome and fulfillment of an unconscious wish, and that unconscious wishes are infantile in source and character. The theory of primary and secondary processes uses a development of the old hypothesis of quantity as a conceptual framework and regards infantile, unconscious wishes as close descendants of affective ideas, and wish-fulfillment in dreams as the end of a process involving psychical excitation belonging to and displaced from such quantitatively regarded wishes. This theory makes use of some hypotheses related to those worked out in the *Project for a Scientific Psychology,* in which "processes which had to be described" in cases of neurosis were explained by being replaced by analogous processes in the central nervous system;[5] the two-processes theory of dreams places its entities and processes in a rather odd locale called the "mental apparatus," which is neither the central nervous system nor the mind or psyche, although it has resemblances to previous conceptions of both. This theory, which I call the wish-fulfillment-quantity theory, was later expanded to cover neurotic symptoms (see, for instance, the *Introductory Lectures* and *New Introductory Lectures*), and was partly modified or overlapped, partly filled out, to cover in more detail the prehistory or predisposing causes of neurosis and its exciting causes in the quantitative libido theory (see, for instance, the metapsychological papers).[6]

In the second direction, Freud attempted in the first instance to develop a theory made up of postulates that were answers to questions that he took his dream-material, gathered or interpreted through "free association," to be asking; he attempted to base the postulates on considerations in or implied by the material. This level or direction of the theory is similar and in many respects parallel to the new theory of idea and quantity, but it does not treat unconscious wishes and wish-fulfillment in explicitly quantitative terms. Wishes are regarded as (a special kind of) desire, wish-fulfillment as (a special kind of) satisfaction or gratification. What I call the wish-fulfillment-mind theory postulates processes involving unconscious wishes, and interaction between parts or aspects of the mind or psyche, to account for the formation of dreams and symptoms and the peculiar characteristics that are ascribed to them. These processes and this interaction are assumed to go on in the mind or psyche, not the "mental apparatus"; they are supposed to be inferred from dreams, their products. The wish-fulfillment-mind theory, first presented in chapters II through V (or VI) of *The Interpretation of Dreams*, was extended to cover neurotic symptoms (*Introductory Lectures*, case histories, etc.) and had the same sort of relation to a not explicitly quantitative version of the libido theory that the theory of primary and secondary processes had to the quantitatively formulated libido theory (case histories again).

My separation of Freud's explicit theory dealing with dreams and its extensions to deal with neurotic symptoms and neurosis into two theories, directions, or levels—in the sense I mean—is contentious in the respect that Freud did not present or regard them as alternative or separate, and hardly as distinct. He considered them, apparently, rather as interlocking halves of one theory: as two levels of one theory in the sense that the quantity-process wish-fulfillment theory explained the processes that were inferred from their results in the wish-fulfillment-mind theory; or as two levels of the same theory in the sense that the wish-fulfillment-mind theory described, classified, correlated, and in one way explained the material in close connection with it, while the quantity-process wish-fulfillment theory provided a further, ultimate explanation in more abstract hypotheses, from, so to speak, a greater height.

But the trouble with the view that the wish-fulfillment-mind and wish-fulfillment-quantity theories are two parts of one theory—its first-level and second-level postulates—is that although the quantity theory seems to explain the wish-fulfillment-mind postulates, or the material as formulated in wish-fulfillment terms, it does so in approximately the way in which the vicissitudes of "cranial excitation," belonging to somatic equivalents of ideas, seemed to explain the vicissitudes ascribed to affect belonging to ideas in Freud's and Breuer's first theoretical formulations: essentially, by duplicating them in another locale. Although the wish-fulfillment-mind level or direction of Freud's theory is not in every respect a parallel, in (compromise) mental terms, to the (compromise) quantitative hypotheses, on the whole it tells the same story in a different arena; that is, it gives another version of processes undergone by the same units and interaction among the same parts, aspects, systems, or agencies of the mental apparatus/psyche/mind. The mental apparatus is an elevated version of the psyche, or the psyche is, perhaps more accurately, a humanized version of the mental apparatus, although things are ascribed to the mental apparatus that could not be ascribed to the mind. Thus I regard the two directions of the theory first presented in *The Interpretation of Dreams* not only as conceptually distinct, but as separate in the sense of being alternative rather than interlocking.

But to regard the two theories as separate in any other way

is perhaps artificial, in the respect that, although they are on the whole presented in different sections of *The Interpretation of Dreams* (Chapter VI making a transition between them) and although some later works (e.g., the metapsychological papers) use the quantity-process version almost exclusively, while others (e.g., the case histories) deal with the material mainly in wish-fulfillment-mind terms, on the other hand some works (e.g., *On Dreams*) shuffle the two theories almost inextricably, while others again (e.g., *Introductory Lectures* or the later *Inhibitions, Symptoms, and Anxiety*) alternate between one theory or level and the other with such rapidity that although one can pick out this passage as "wish-fulfillment-mind" and that as "wish-fulfillment-quantity"—and the other as "mixed"— there can hardly be said to be a substantial separation. Even in *The Interpretation of Dreams,* the wish-fulfillment-mind theory is set up so as to allow for easy transposition into quantitative terms, and Freud in presenting it sometimes goes off into such terms, or quantity-level considerations or formulations are put down in a nonquantitative context. In the first—and later— presentation of the quantity version, these points hold in reverse. Also, although the two levels or theories can be regarded as having been formulated in different ways—the wish-fulfillment-mind version in closer connection with the material, the quantity theory in closer connection with the old framework and theory of quantity—I cannot say to what extent they were worked out separately, e.g., at different times.

I regard the two theories as having influenced one another, although again this is something of a simplification. It would be quite correct, I think, to say that the considerations Freud put forward to support his wish-fulfillment-mind postulates had some degree of influence on the neoquantitative postulates, and that the theoretical framework and a model developed in the quantity version heavily influenced the wish-fulfillment postulates.[7]

1. QUANTITATIVE VERSION

A. Two Systems

Excitation arises in the mental apparatus from external and internal sources: stimuli and somatic needs. An excess of excitation is felt as unpleasure, while a return to level is felt as pleasure. In its original state, the mental apparatus is geared simply to the discharge of excess excitation. The first endeavor of the apparatus is to get rid of excitation through the kind of motor activity known as expression of emotion. (The hungry baby kicks and screams.) Then, following an experience of satisfaction (e.g., the mother's bringing nourishment) a link is set up between the mnemic images of the perception of satisfaction and of the excitation in question. When next the need arises, excitation builds up to the point of being felt as unpleasure, and as a result of the link between memory-traces, an impulse appears that seeks to reevoke the perception of satisfaction. Such an impulse is called a wish. (A primitive wish is also called a path to a memory-trace, ready to be traversed by fresh excitation at any time, and a "current in the apparatus starting from unpleasure and aiming at pleasure.")[8] The reappearance of the perception of satisfaction is the fulfillment of the wish, but in the primitive mental apparatus no distinction is made between the mnemic image of a perception of satisfaction and an actual experience of satisfaction. Wishing thus consists of the cathexis of a mnemic image. That is, in the infant, wishing ends in hallucinating.

The attempt to get rid of excitation through motor activity—the expression of emotion—is not successful if the excitation continues to accumulate (and be felt as unpleasure) as fast as it is discharged, as is the case if its source is a somatic need. And the primary, hallucinatory wishing is unsuccessful (unless it is "maintained unceasingly") for the same reason.

It becomes necessary for a way to be found of distinguishing between the mnemic image of a perception of satisfaction and its actual perception. To this end a process of reality-testing is instituted. The apparatus becomes capable of tolerating and holding in check amounts of excitation, sending out small portions of them in reality-testing or thought-activity, and finally releasing them in deliberate motor activity designed to bring about that change in external reality that will provide satisfaction. In short, though still aiming at pleasure, the apparatus may now be said to operate under the "reality principle." The route to wish-fulfillment is now more round-about, but more sure of success.

The transition from primary to secondary process is not, however, complete. There remain "at the core of our being" many leftover, indestructible, infantile wishes. The mental apparatus under the secondary process is unable to deal with these wishes because it is unable to cathect any idea from which it cannot inhibit a discharge in the direction of the release of unpleasure.

Under the primary process, in contrast, the metal apparatus "pursues an ostrich policy" and can do *nothing* but wish. This is the case with some of the infantile wishes, the cathexis or fulfillment of which would now lead to unpleasure rather than pleasure, and, therefore, they are disregarded and left to their own devices. Not being incorporated into the body of ideas subject to the secondary process, the whole group of leftover infantile wishes remains subject to the primary process. Thus in the mental apparatus of the adult there are two bodies or systems of ideas. Those ideas—wishes—subject to the primary process may become conscious only under extraordinary circumstances, and their system may be called the System Ucs. The ideas subject to the secondary process may under ordinary circumstances become conscious; theirs is the System Pcs.

B. The Formation of Dreams and Neurotic Symptoms

The leftover, disregarded, but indestructible infantile wishes remain under the control of the primary process, and thus their aim is just discharge. With this aim, they may transfer their excitation (or their "wishful force" or "intensity") onto preconscious thoughts. The system in which these thoughts arose, still unable to inhibit the development of unpleasure, withdraws its cathexis from transference thoughts as it withdraws cathexis from the unconscious wishes from which they have received extra excitation. Thus, on the one hand the transference thoughts are "drawn into the Ucs.," and on the other hand they are abandoned by the Pcs. It may also happen that a preconscious thought is from its inception linked to an unconscious wish and thus never receives preconscious cathexis; or that a preconscious thought may temporarily receive added force from the Ucs.

Once linked with the Ucs. and abandoned by the Pcs., transference thoughts become subject to the primary process. "Their one aim is motor discharge, or, if the path is open, hallucinatory revival of the desired perceptual identity" or to "force their way through with their excitation."[9]

A dream is formed under two conditions: first, the relaxation of the Pcs. system, its concentration upon the wish to sleep, or the relaxation of the "censorship" which ordinarily prevents the passage of unconscious wishes from their own domain; second, the occurrence of certain transformations among the transference thoughts, in accordance with the primary process. "The intensities of the individual ideas become capable of discharge *en bloc* and pass over from one idea to another, so that certain ideas are formed which are endowed with great intensity";[10] the intensity of a whole train of thought may eventually be concentrated in a single ideational element.[11] Because of the freedom with which intensities are transferred, "intermediate ideas," "composite structures," or "compromises" may be formed. The ideas between which intensities are transferred may be related by very loose associational links: "in particular, we find associations based on homonyms and verbal similarities treated as equal in value to the rest."[12] Ideas that are mutually contradictory may be lumped together in condensations or compromises.

These transformations are antithetical to the working of the secondary process, or system Pcs., which seeks to find "the 'right' ideational element,"[13] and which would be impeded in its rational working by permitting such condensations as these just mentioned. But they serve the purpose—discharge—of the Ucs. "The outcome of the activity of condensation is the achievement of the intensities required for forcing a way through into the perceptual systems."[14] In the transformations just mentioned—the dream work—"the whole stress is laid upon making the cathecting energy mobile and capable of discharge; the content and proper meaning of the psychical elements to which the cathexes are attached are treated as of little consequence."[15] In this way preconscious thoughts, the vehicles of unconscious excitation, which individually would be prevented from emerging into consciousness, finally achieve their aim.

In the formation of a neurotic symptom, a process very similar to that of the dream-work takes place. There are two central differences. In addition to the concentration of intensities upon a few ideas, a second condition allows a dream to occur—that is, the relaxation of the Pcs. system, or its concentration upon the wish to sleep; whereas the second condition in the outbreak of a neurotic symptom is the extra-intensity of the unconscious wishes—the amount of excitation, freely transferable, in the Ucs. The second difference is that in the formation of a neurotic symptom there is invariably a contribution from the Pcs., when it cannot prevent an unconscious wish from forcing a way through: a symptom is a compromise between an unconscious wish and a defensive impulse of the Pcs.

The theory of primary and secondary processes, which seeks mainly to account for the formation of dreams, symptoms, and other products of the unconscious within the context of a view of mental functioning in general, is partly overlapped and partly supplemented by the libido theory, which seeks mainly to account for the genesis—the prehistory and exciting causes—of neurosis within the context of a view of the development of the sexual instinct. In order to fill out Freud's mature theory, it is useful to add it here.

The libido theory turns on an application of the hypothesis of quantity to the person as a whole; that is, a view of the person as containing a total quantity of libido (psychical sexual energy—or the energetic component of the sexual instinct, or the force by which it seeks discharge—which is correlated with somatic energy, arising from processes of excitation in erogenous zones of the body), which as a whole may increase or decrease in amount, become strangulated or, in effect, displaced, and be discharged. Thus: libido, or the sexual instinct, develops through a series of organizations from infancy to adulthood, i.e., the oral, anal, phallic, and genital, each step characterized by the primacy of a certain component instinct or impulse, having one or more aims and objects. It may happen that parts of the total quantity of libido are left behind in the course of development, fixated in pregenital (infantile) organizations or upon early (Oedipal) objects. Fixation may occur because of some innate or constitutional imbalance, or overstrength of a given component-instinct in relation to others, or because of certain childhood experiences or fantasies that have led to excessive stimulation or gratification. The total quantity that goes on to develop in the normal manner, toward the primacy of the genital impulse and the adoption of certain aims and objects, is thus weakened. The exciting cause of neurosis is typically a privation (e.g., the loss of an erotic object); its immediate effect in any case is the strangulation or damming-up of libido, lacking a sufficient outlet. Accumulating, libido flows back or regresses to the point or points of fixation. If there is repression at the point of fixation, a conflict ensues between the sexual instinct seeking an infantile satisfaction, or the reinforced infantile impulses seeking to force a way through, and the defensive impulses of the Ego, or its reinforcement of the barriers of anticathexes; such a conflict leads to the production of neurotic symptoms.[16]

2. MIND VERSION

A. Two Mentalities

There are two types of mentality in every person, which may be called the unconscious-infantile and the (pre-) conscious-adult.[17]

The unconscious is the child living on in the adult. It is infantile in substance—its bedrock, at least, being composed of wishes left over from childhood, wishes for satisfactions that were once enjoyed, or that were fantasized in childhood. Because old desires are put away in the unconscious, there remaining indestructible and, as it were, left on their own, the unconscious can be considered a *part* of the person, almost a place in his mind. It is equally, however, an aspect of the person, and a type of mentality. It is infantile in style as well as in substance.

As a child may be said to have intense desires (many of them springing from somatic sources) and little if any ability to forgo an immediate demand for satisfaction, or to plan, or consider the means to his ends, and as he promptly and simply expresses his desires, or imagines their fulfillment, rather than considering *how* to satisfy them in reality, so the childish part of the person behaves.

The adult part or aspect, on the contrary, does not consist only in wishes. The adult mentality thinks, plans, and considers, with a view to the eventual satisfaction of its wishes through a modification of external reality. Whereas the unconscious or infantile aspect is a hotbed of desires, the preconscious system, second agency, or Ego has learned to pay attention to the considerations of self-preservation. It is the part that gets educated and civilized, and in contrast to the unconscious-infantile is moralizing and aesthetic, as well as prudent. Thus many of the satisfactions that were once enjoyed would no longer be pleasing to this aspect of the person, and it does not desire them, although the lowest stratum still does.

The unconscious is primary in the sense that it is prior to the development of the adult mentality and in the sense that the preconscious-realistic-adult is an overlay. It can only—at best—cope with, and usefully channel, the unconscious wishes.

The adult aspect and the buried I-want-I-want do not mingle, except in the respect that the latter, attempting in its own style to intrude, be expressed, be satisfied, may effect a translation of its wishes into preconscious thoughts (or a sub-stitution of the latter for the former). The adult Ego keeps it-self dissociated, leaves the infantile wishes to their own devices, and cuts itself off from any transference thoughts or wishes. It is as if there were a barrier or an endopsychic cen-sorship that, under normal circumstances in the waking adult, prevents altogether the emergence of unconscious (first-agency) wishes to satisfaction or expression. Where the barrier is considered as "the censorship," it can be said to represent the power of the second agency, or Ego, which controls access to motor activity and consciousness.

B. Formation of Dreams and Neurotic
Symptoms

Dreams and neurotic symptoms represent the predominance, or breakthrough, of the infantile aspect.

The manifest content of a dream—that is, the dream as dreamt (and reported)—usually seems incoherent, nonsensical, and pointless. But when it is considered in the light of the dreamer's free associations—that is, everything that occurs to him when he asks himself what each separate element of the dream calls to mind, without attempting to judge the dream as a whole, and without holding back anything that occurs to him as frivolous, irrelevant, or embarrassing, or otherwise what he would prefer not to mention—then the dream can be found to have a meaning.[18] And its meaning is the fulfillment of an unconscious wish of the dreamer's.

The dreamer's free associations are considered to be the same as the dream-thoughts, or latent content of the dream; but again they are considered as "shafts" dug down to the more complex tunnels of the latent thoughts.

The manifest dream is a translation of the latent thoughts into a new form of expression; or a substitute for the latent content; the shape in which the dream-wish is expressed; the thought ("as a rule of something that is wished") "objectified, represented as a scene, or, as it seems to us, . . . experienced"; or, in general, the unrecognizable representation of a wish as fulfilled.[19]

The question why a dream did not "say what it meant straight out" (or, "what is the origin of the remarkable . . . form in which the wish-fulfillment is expressed")[20] is to be answered in terms of the wishes that dreams fulfill, and the relations between the two aspects of the person.

The desires satisfied in dreams are "repressed" wishes ["there is a simultaneous inhibition which holds them down"] . . . which belong to the first system and whose fulfillment is opposed by the second system,"[21] or they are such that there is an inclination to put up a defense against them, or they have grounds for fearing the censorship. The manifest dream does not obviously display the character of gratifying a first-agency wish. Its indirection, or incomprehensibility, must be considered a disguise or distortion necessitated by the endopsychic censorship.

In correspondence with the Ego's concentration on the wish to sleep, the censorship is somewhat relaxed: better a fantasmal, substitutive, incomprehensible fulfillment of an alien wish than the clamor of the unfulfilled wish for expression and satisfaction.

The relations between the latent and manifest content can be elucidated in terms of "displacement." In general, a given, manifest idea or element takes on the psychical significance or wishful force of another; or replaces, stands for, or represents another, which is of greater emotional interest; or, the manifest element is a substitute, cover, or disguise for the other; or, an indifferent idea takes the place of one that is psychically significant through a displacement of "psychical emphasis." The manifest element is not always quite indifferent to itself. In certain instances, for example, an "affect that has grounds for avoiding the censorship" may "slip in, as it were, under the wing" of a "similar, legitimate affect arising from a permissible source."[22] In dreams, and in neurotic symptoms, affects generally remain unaltered, while an ideational content may be replaced by another; in these productions "an affect is always justified," although "the idea which belongs to it . . . has been repressed and replaced by a substitute."[23]

The latent thoughts are in more than one layer or level; the wish that the analysis first reveals a dream (or neurotic symptom) as fulfilling may itself be a displacement (substitute, cover) for another. Thus a dream (or neurotic symptom) may have a series of meanings; a series of wish-fulfillments are superimposed on one another, "the bottom one being the fulfillment of a wish dating from earliest childhood."[24]

It is possible for a dream to have, as well as a series of meanings (layer behind layer), a group of meanings on any one level, and this is the rule in the case of neurotic symptoms. These, which come about not through a relaxation of the censorship but in spite of a build-up in the defenses against its emergence, carry to a greater extent than (most) dreams the mark of the Ego. While primarily the gratification of an infantile wish (one the satisfaction of which would be displeasing to the Ego) a neurotic symptom manifests the second agency's attitude of it-shall-not-pass, not only in the substitutive, distorted character of the wish-fulfillment, but also by fulfilling a counter-wish of defensive impulse at the same time, and generally in the same manifest content. For instance, a hysterical girl satisfies an old, unconscious wish to be constantly pregnant through hysterical vomiting. But since the symptom threatens to spoil her attractive appearance, it also fulfills a defensive, self-punitive impulse. The neurotic symptom is thus a compromise between the two aspects of the person.

The neurotic or the dreamer perceives or experiences what is a substitute for that which the infantile part of him desires; the desire is thereby gratified—but in such a way as to placate that part of him which tries to prevent the passage of such a wish to consciousness, or issue in motor activity, or satisfaction. A neurotic symptom, by also gratifying a wish of the adult, prudent, moralizing aspect, renders the infantile satisfaction tolerable to the adult system in another respect.

The libido theory can, in part, be taken as a classification of desires (with points as to their development and relation to one another) under the headings of "instincts," which in this sense of the theory need not be considered as having a quantitative component.

The quantitative view of nosogenesis has also a counterpart without the quantity. This is the view that the precondition of neurosis is a store of unconscious, infantile desires (instigated or aroused by childhood experiences or fantasies, remaining indestructible in the unconscious), and that its exciting cause is a privation—or a difficulty in adult life, a problem in dealing with reality, or a current conflict—in the face of which the subject retreats or regresses by way of preconscious fantasies (long tolerated by the Ego, censorship, or forces of defense because they were not very strong) to the infantile desires, which are thereby revived and press importunately for expression, consciousness, and satisfaction. Their pressing forward and the Ego's or adult aspect's renewed attempts to prevent their emergence constitute the neurotic conflict, the issue of which is symptoms.

The second-level view of cure may be added here: it is that neurotic symptoms are removed by making the unconscious wishes conscious; they then cease to be indestructible, crumbling away like buried things when exposed to light and air, or being incorporated into the Ego.

3. PERSISTENCE

Freud regarded his material—increased in scope and depth, partly through his application of the method of "free association"—from the point of view of his old theoretical framework of idea and quantity, and through the filter of the picture contained in the previous theory of repression and consequent symptom-formation by conversion or displacement. The theory of primary and secondary processes and its later developments quite directly reflects the old picture—in spite of the shift in central concepts that it incorporates.

Consider first the wish-fulfillment-quantity theory as a reflection—or modification and expansion—of the previous quantity framework and theory.

A. The basic part of the "hypothesis of quantity"—the assumption that an affective idea has two components, an idea (paradigm: memory of event) and a sum of affect or excitation, attached or belonging to or occupying the idea—is reflected in the new hypothesis that an infantile wish consists in the cathexis, i.e., occupation, of a mnemic image—the memory-trace of an experience of satisfaction—by a quantity of psychical excitation (arising, in the paradigm case, from a somatic need). This means, in the theory of primary and secondary processes, that infantile wishing is hallucinating.[25]

B. The remainder of the hypothesis of quantity—that the sum of affect or excitation belonging to an idea is capable of increase or decrease, may become separated from the idea and then is capable of displacement onto a substitute idea (or conversion into a somatic innervation), can be discharged (and, if too great to be contained, requires discharge)—is reflected in new, more complicated hypotheses. (1) Excitation belonging to infantile wishes, or within the infantile mental apparatus, is capable of increase

66

through continuance of a need or non-satisfaction; decrease short of reduction to level, e.g., through partial discharge in random motor activity—which, with hallucinatory wishing, is the response in the infantile mental apparatus to excess excitation, which is felt as unpleasure—and restoration to level (discharge), which is felt as pleasure, through satisfaction in reality (an actual experience of satisfaction), which cuts off the influx of excitation. The infantile mental apparatus responds to excess excitation, felt as unpleasure, in automatic attempts to slough it off, or in other words is governed by the sole and simple principle of seeking immediately to discharge its excitation. (It is therefore not adapted to securing satisfaction in reality.)[26] (2) Within the mental apparatus of the adult, some infantile wishes remain preserved and form the core of the System Ucs. The unconscious-infantile system remains subject to the primary process, or the pleasure (immediate attempted discharge) principle. Toward their sole aim of discharge, quantities within the Ucs. are capable of free displacement onto other ideas within the Ucs. or onto ideas originated in the System Pcs.—that is, the system of ideas, adult in origin and character, that, unlike the unconscious wishes and their ex-preconscious vehicles (which, when cathected with excitation from the Ucs., become themselves unconscious), are normally, in ordinary circumstances, capable, at any time, of becoming conscious.[27]

Besides the assimilation of unconscious affective ideas to unconscious, infantile wishes (excess excitation/unpleasure) and of discharge, or reduction of excitation to level, to pleasure/satisfaction, the theory of primary and secondary processes takes a new departure mainly in postulating *two* principles governing the disposal of psychical excitation. The primary, pleasure, or immediate discharge principle guides the unconscious-infantile system, part, aspect, or mentality within the adult mental apparatus. The secondary, reality, economy, or delayed discharge principle guides the preconscious-adult system. Here, amounts of excitation are held in check, small portions are expended in (rational) thought-activity and reality-testing (to distinguish, as the Ucs. cannot, between mnemic image of satisfaction and satisfaction in reality), and finally greater portions are released in purposeful motor activity designed to bring about actual satisfaction. Preconscious excitation is not allowed free displacement, which would disrupt rational thought and hence actual satisfaction.[28]

C. The old theoretical postulate that neurotic symptoms are caused by the displacement or conversion of affect or excitation torn away from an idea when, meeting opposition from the Ego and driven by a force of defense, it is deprived of its affect and made unconscious is reflected in the central postulates of the new quantity theory.

i. The old view that ideas, meeting a force of defense from the Ego, are deprived of their affective component or sum of excitation, thus becoming weak or being made unconscious, is reflected in the new postulates that the System Pcs. (subject to the secondary process) withholds its cathexis (excitation or attention) from the leftover infantile wishes, so that they are incapable ordinarily, or in normal circumstances, of becoming conscious or of being expressed or satisfied, and does so because the Pcs. is unable to prevent the release of unpleasure in the event of the infantile wishes' emergence; and that it withdraws its cathexis from preconscious ideas that have received excitation from the infantile wishes and have thus been drawn into the Ucs. and become subject to the primary process— with the same result. Besides withholding or withdrawing its excitation, the adult-preconscious also places anticathexes or counter-forces—or, it maintains a barrier—in the way of unconscious wishes and their ex-preconscious vehicles to block their emergence to consciousness, expression, or satisfaction.[29]

ii. The old view that neurotic symptoms are caused by the conversion or displacement of excitation removed from affective ideas when they are repressed—the excitation seeking discharge, and unable to obtain it by normal means because of separation from ideational content and because of a defensive counter-force—is reflected in the new postulate that a precondition for the formation of dreams, neurotic symptoms, and other pathogenic structures is a body of infantile wishes, which are unable to achieve normal expression or satisfaction because of their being left alone or put aside and blocked by the dominant system, and because, being governed by the primary principle or subject to the primary process, they aim solely and simply at immediate discharge: they tend simply to force a way through or to achieve motor discharge or hallucinatory revival of perceptual identity.[30]

iii. The old view that neurotic symptoms are formed by the conversion or displacement of quantities of excitation removed from affective ideas when they are repressed is further reflected in the new postulate that sums of excitation in the Ucs. (belonging to infantile wishes) are capable, in their search for immediate discharge, of being displaced or transferred en bloc on to preconscious thoughts, some of which thereby become vehicles or substitutes for the unconscious wishes, and that through this displacement dreams and neurotic symptoms are formed; they are a special kind of wish-fulfillment, abnormal in the waking adult, which is occasioned in part by the lack or removal of one sort of excitation and brought about through the concentrated displacement of the other sort of excitation.[31]

The concept of a special, primary kind of wish-fulfillment is at the center of the theory, but the account of how a dream or symptom fulfills an unconscious wish is not very clear: two answers seem to be offered.

One answer is that a dream or neurotic symptom can be said to constitute the satisfaction of an unconscious wish in that the excitation of or belonging to the wish, displaced onto a group of preconscious thoughts in accordance with the policy of discharge at any price (the excitation will out), and then concentrated on a few of these thoughts, almost regardless of their content or proper meaning or relations, succeeds in its sole endeavor—i.e., to force a way through.

The other answer is that because an unconscious wish is a quantity of excitation, arising from a particular source and directed toward, or cathecting, the mnemic image of a satisfaction—that is, something (to be) desired—when *that* quantity of excitation becomes attached to a group of transference thoughts and finally, in concentration, onto a few such thoughts, the latter become replacements or substitutes for the original as that which is desired. (Hence excitation is sometimes, e.g., in Chapter VI, referred to as "wishful force.") The Ucs. makes no distinction between (mnemic) image of satisfaction and actual perception or experience. Thus when transference ideas so conceived surface in a dream—are perceived—then an unconscious wish is being, in a manner both primary and indirect, satisfied. The dream is a hallucinatory revival, not indeed of the unconscious idea or memory (wish), but of its stand-in or replacement. Unconscious excitation plays the dual role of translating an unconscious wish into preconscious thoughts (or turning the latter into stand-ins or replacements for the former) and of pushing some of them forward to the point of expression or consciousness.[32]

iv. The old view that what is antithetical to and opposed by the Ego is equivalent to that which is pathogenic (and resisted, unconscious, and repressed) is maintained, with modifications and additions, in the new theory. The System Pcs., being the system of normal adult thoughts (and/or the normal adult mentality; that is, operating in the normal adult manner) and being the dominant system, itself capable of achieving consciousness in normal circumstances and controlling access to consciousness, holding down the unconscious wishes and their ex-preconscious vehicles, is in effect the Ego—and is soon explicitly identified as the Ego.[33] The preconscious-adult system of ideas, or mentality, is now assumed to have no contact with the infantile-unconscious (later, the Id), but to inhibit its emergence systematically because of the unpleasure that *would* be released should the fundamental-unconscious achieve consciousness or satisfaction. The two aspects, parts, systems, or agencies are not only distinct, but separate. Conflict between the two systems is precisely the attempts of one to break through and of the other systematically to prevent its emergence. Dreams and neurotic symptoms are ascribed almost entirely to the characteristic efforts of the unconscious-infantile to force a way through. The role of the preconscious-adult is wholly negative or defensive. The Pcs. plays a role in dream-formation by somewhat relaxing the barrier that it ordinarily keeps up to block the Ucs. from emergence (the barrier is relaxed because the Ego or adult system is concentrated on the wish to sleep) and, on the other hand, by maintaining the barrier to the extent of (usually) preventing the direct emergence of the infantile, unconscious wishes. The Pcs. plays a part in the formation of neurotic symptoms first by strengthening the barrier against the Ucs.—which, increased in force by a regression of excitation, is striving with exceptional strength to break through—and then, when partially overcome by the seeking of unconscious excitation for discharge (expression, satisfaction), both by maintaining its counter-force to the extent of preventing the direct emergence of the unconscious wishes and by adding a palliative, or satisfaction for itself, to the expression of those wishes in a neurotic symptom. A neurotic symptom is primarily an outbreak of overflowing excitation from the Ucs. and/or an indirect satisfaction of an unconscious, infantile, Ego-incompatible, still partially Ego-blocked wish.[34]

D. Other respects in which the quantity theory of Freud's maturity reflects the picture contained in his previous theory of quantity could be set out, but it may be more useful here to insist that the theory of primary and secondary processes and its later modifications and elaborations maintain the central aspects of the old picture. First, the shift from affective ideas to wishes and from conversion or displacement in search for discharge to wish-fulfillment is by no means complete. The neoquantitative conceptions of "unconscious wishes" and "wish-fulfillment" are compromise-conceptions incorporating the older concepts of affective ideas and strangulation-discharge. Freud's new view of wishes and wish-fulfillment is such as to fit into the picture contained in the previous quantity theory. In developing the point that a hysterical attack is not merely a "discharge," but an "action," or that neurotic symptoms and dreams are essentially "wish-fulfillments," Freud makes them differ from other acts and other satisfactions as being the end results of processes tending to discharge.

Second, the old view of the psyche as divided into parts or aspects—the discharge-seeking, repressed Unconscious on one hand, the defensive Ego on the other—the identification of the pathogenic with that which is incompatible with the Ego (repressed-unconscious), and the view of the Ego as involved only in a defensive way in the formation of neurotic symptoms is not only reflected but maintained and elaborated and, so to speak, toughened in the new quantity theory.

Finally, to put these two points together, it seems fair to say that the new quantity theory—which treats unconscious wishes, but not preconscious thoughts, as mnemic images cathected with sums of psychical excitation; which regards the system of unconscious wishes, but not the system of preconscious thoughts, as reacting automatically to the increase or decrease (excess or lack) of excitation, as subject to free displacement of excitation, and as under the necessity of attempting immediate discharge; and which attributes the presence of such non-normal "structures" as dreams and neurotic symptoms mainly to the strangulation and attempted discharge of excitation belonging to the unconscious-infantile wishes, the preconscious-adult-Ego-thoughts ("defensive impulses") being involved only as counter-force—revitalizes the old hypothesis of quantity by extending it and at the same time limiting its scope; it sets aside the unconscious wishes left over from childhood and the productions it attributes to them as precisely the phenomena that the hypothesis, extended, can cover.

4. REFLECTIONS

A. Consider now the wish–fulfillment–mind theory as a reflection of the picture developed in the new quantity theory from the old framework and theory with some new material. The wish–fulfillment–mind theory does parallel the new quantity theory, more closely in some versions than in others. The wish–fulfillment–mind postulates as first developed in Chapters II through V of *The Interpretation of Dreams* do not precisely parallel the postulates regarding quantity processes in the "mental apparatus" that are developed in Chapter VII. The main points of divergence from the parallel in the first part of the book are these.

    i. Freud implies, or states, in developing the wish–fulfillment–mind theory that the Ego, second agency, or adult aspect (compare the System Pcs. in the quantity theory) has *specific* objections to particular first-agency wishes, that it puts up defenses against or bans wishes that are unpleasing to it or that it objects to, and that it modifies the realization or expression of these wishes "as it thinks fit," to the point at which the expression is so distorted as to be unrecognizable and therefore unobjectionable.[35] This implies that the second agency's inhibition of first-agency wishes is not like a wholesale, systematic withdrawal of attention or awareness and placement of barriers, and that "unconscious wishes," while described in strict parallel to the quantity theory as inadmissable to consciousness, are not separated from contact with the second agency. The second agency *is aware* of first-agency wishes, and they are not unconscious in the sense of being unknown—which the wish–fulfillment–quantity theory would have them to be.

    ii. The conclusion that all dreams are ultimately fulfillments of *infantile* wishes, and that the core of the first, "creative" agency is infantile wishes, is more tentative in the questions and answers of the first part of *The Interpretation of*

Dreams than in Chapter VII, and is not reached even tentatively until late in the first presentation of the wish-fulfillment theory; the infantile character of the Unconscious is not central in the theory as first presented.

iii. In the wish-fulfillment-mind postulates as first presented, the incomprehensibility or "distortion" of "manifest dreams" is put down wholly (until the transitional Chapter VI, and even there in principle) to censorship or defense exercised by the second agency upon wishes of the first agency. In the wish-fulfillment-quantity theory, although the barriers erected by the System Pcs. against the emergence of wishes or excitation belonging to the Ucs. are stressed, the peculiar character of the "wish-fulfillment" is ascribed mainly to the peculiar, primary process of the Ucs. or its principle of immediate attempts to dispose of excitation rising above the unpleasure level: its striving, toward the end of discharge, for "hallucinatory revival of perceptual identity" or "motor discharge" and its capacity to transfer sums of excitation "en bloc" on to ex-preconscious vehicle thoughts—regardless of their "content or proper meaning"—and re-transfer until some among the mass of "transference thoughts" gain the necessary strength to "force a way through" to the "perceptual systems," or to consciousness and expression.

By the same token, the whole emphasis in Chapters II through V is on the meaning of dreams—on the view that dreams are formed in order to "represent a wish as fulfilled," and that wishes are the motives of dreams—while in Chapter VII, unconscious wishes are regarded as more like causes than like motives, meaning is hardly mentioned, and a dream is regarded not so much as representing a wish as fulfilled, but as allowing its excitation to "force a way through," or as allowing thoughts that have received its cathexis to be "represented," i.e., represented by some among them, and hallucinated.

B. The wish-fulfillment-mind theory never becomes a strict parallel in every respect to the new wish-fulfillment-quantity theory. But, in its most official presentations—for instance, as summed up in Chapters VI and VII of *The Interpretation of Dreams* and presented in *On Dreams* and the *Introductory Lectures*—it is made to approach the quantity-process picture more closely than it does in Chapters II through V.

i. It becomes Freud's official position, stated in nonquantitative terms, that the second agency, Ego, or adult aspect cuts itself off from the first agency or Unconscious (later, the Id), ignores it and leaves it alone, has no contact with it, and sets up systematic defenses or a censorship that quite prevents it, except in the extraordinary circumstances of dreaming and neurosis, from achieving expression or satisfaction and, even in these circumstances, prevents it itself from being admitted to consciousness: the Unconscious is unconscious, not known.[36]

ii. It is Freud's official nonquantitative position that the precondition of neurosis and dreams is a store of infantile wishes remaining in the adult, and that such wishes are the core of the Unconscious. The quantity-theory postulate that there are two systems, Ucs. and Pcs., and two principles of discharge, one governing the infantile wishes and the other the preconscious thoughts, is paralleled by the wish-fulfillment-mind postulate that there are two parts or aspects of the person, mind or psyche, and two types of mentality or ways of functioning: the first agency, Id, or infantile aspect is unconscious, consists basically in infantile wishes, and has an infantile mode of expression; the second agency, Ego, or adult aspect consists in the adult's ideas, operates rationally and realistically, and is (at least largely) preconscious.[37]

The quantity-level postulate that the infantile-Ucs. operates under a principle of simple discharge, by the nearest means and without check except from outside itself (or, operates under the pleasure principle), is reflected in the wish-fulfillment-mind version that the unconscious part, aspect, mentality *is* infantile: the Unconscious, first agency, or Id is the child living on in the adult, and like a child is selfish, amoral, non-aesthetic, imprudent, and irrational, and consists in intense but unrealistic wishes.[38] The unconscious mentality is childlike in demanding immediate satisfaction and expressing its wishes or imagining satisfaction (accepting substitutive and/or phantasmal satisfaction) rather than considering how best to satisfy its desires in reality and taking steps to do so.[39]

The quantity view of the Pcs. as governed by the reality principle—as saving its excitation and using it to bring about actual satisfaction after rational thought-activity and reality-testing—is closely reflected in the wish-fulfillment-mind view of the preconscious-adult aspect as not consisting wholly in wishes, as thinking, planning, and considering toward the end of actual satisfaction, and as exercising self-control and self-preservation, being prudent, moralizing, and aesthetic, and becoming civilized and educated.[40]

iii. In the most official presentations of the wish-fulfillment-mind theory, there is emphasis—as implied in the preceding points—on the concept of a mode of expression or process of formation of dreams and symptoms that is peculiar to the first agency or Unconscious and that is childlike or "primary" in character. There are within the wish-fulfillment-mind theory (or there are, stated in not directly quantitative terms) two ways of regarding dream-formation and two ways of answering the question of *how* a dream fulfills a wish.

The first view is that a dream, motivated by a wish of the first agency and formed in accordance with a meaning of the first agency, through a process of translation or encoding in which certain elements or ideas come to take the place of or become substitutes or covers for the original meaning (ideas, wish)—this translation being necessitated (and, apparently, accomplished) by the censorious, defensive second agency in order to make the dream incomprehensible—is decoded through the dreamer's "associations" and found to represent a wish of the dreamer's (first agency's) as fulfilled and to contain or express his precedent meaning. Freud does not in connection with his exposition of this view explain exactly how a dream is supposed to fulfill a wish. The formulations that most closely fit this view are presented later than it and are not themselves altogether clear. Piecing together several remarks, the nearest approach to an answer seems to be this: the comparatively indifferent and innocuous translation-thoughts are taken as covers or substitutes for the subject's (first agency's) wish or his precedent meaning, which is that x is the case (x being something desired, or the fulfillment of a wish), and the substitute thoughts are presented as a scene that is experienced by the subject "as if it were reality." Or, the dreamer's precedent meaning or thought, which is "in the optative," ("So that x were the case") is replaced by substitute thoughts, which are presented in the "straightforward present," so that (A) the manifest dream says "y is the case" and means or stands for the thought "x is the case," and (B) since "the thought is presented as an immediate situation with the 'perhaps' omitted,"[41] it seems to the dreamer that what means or stands for the fulfillment of his wish *is* the case. (And the precedent meaning or first-agency wish that is recovered first in the course of interpretation is itself a cover, substitute, translation, or derivative of a fundamental-unconscious wish left over from infancy, so that what means or is a substitute for the satisfaction of the first-recovered wish is a substitute, at another remove, for the satisfaction of an infantile wish from the core of the Unconscious.)

The second view of dream-formation and how a dream fulfills a wish is presented in the transitional Chapter VI: a dream is formed by a process of displacement of psychical intensity, emphasis, value, or interest among a body of dream-thoughts in which those that are of greatest interest are stripped of their value, and others that are intrinsically indifferent are given new value by over-determination—having the greatest number of links among the body of dream-thoughts, they receive concentrated intensity—until the chosen ideas become sufficiently intense to be able to take a place in the dream. "The consequence of the displacement is that the dream-content no longer resembles the core of the dream-thoughts and that the dream gives no more than a distortion of the dream-wish which exists in the unconscious. . . . *Is fecit cui profuit*. We may assume, then, that dream displacement comes about through the influence of . . . the censorship of endopsychic defense."[42] According to this second version, a dream "represents" the "dream-thoughts" in the sense that it includes a few of them and pictorializes or "objectifies" them, or presents them as images or as a scene. It is perhaps even more unclear in this version of the wish-fulfillment-mind theory (or transition from it to the quantity theory) than it is in the quantity version just how a dream is supposed to fulfill a wish. Apparently a (first-level) unconscious wish either is implicit in and the center of the "dream-thoughts" or gives rise or intensity (value, etc.) to them; hence, either the emergence of thoughts carrying its intensity or value satisfies its need for emergence (expression), or the displacement of all that intensity or interest belonging to dream-thoughts centering around (or themselves given interest or value by) the dream-wish onto a few of the dream-thoughts converts them into substitutes or vehicles for the wish, so that when they surface—"objectified"—the wish is substitutively and pictorially fulfilled. (And presumably a fundamental-unconscious, infantile wish may have approximately the same relation to the first-recovered wish, or the dream-thoughts, that the first-level wish has to the dream-thoughts.)[43]

Although this second view of dream-formation and dream-satisfaction is clearly closely reflective of the quantity-theory version, the first, more thoroughly "wish-fulfillment" view can also be said to reflect the quantity picture, but at another remove and in somewhat closer relation to the material of observation. The same is true regarding the variant versions of the relationships and interaction between the two agencies, and of their character.

C. It may be noted that the variations within the wish-fulfillment-mind theory—its divergence in some formulations from the quantity picture and its closer approach to the parallel in other versions—involve Freud in contradictions and difficulties of various kinds. For example:

i. The view implied in the first presentation of the wish-fulfillment-mind theory, that "unconscious wishes" are not unknown and are barred from direct expression for specific objectionability, is further implied in many later applications of the theory, e.g. to symptoms; it is always in conflict with what remains Freud's official position, that such wishes are left aside, ignored, systematically banned or buried, out of contact with the preconscious system, and inadmissible to consciousness.

ii. Not only a shift in emphasis is involved in the noncentrality of the conception of the Unconscious (first agency) as basically infantile in the wish-fulfillment theory as first developed and its centrality in the new quantity theory and in parallel wish-fulfillment formulations. In the developing wish-fulfillment-mind theory and in its application, Freud often wants to hold that the "distortion" of "a dream" is accountable in terms of the second agency's dislike of or displeasure in the wishes supposed to be satisfied on first analysis—that is, the wishes attributed to the subject on the basis of the first "interpretation" which provides a dream-report with a meaning. But in formulations that more closely reflect the quantity theory, Freud wants to hold that it is the core-unconscious, infantile wishes which are guarded against by the second agency or adult aspect: the "transference thoughts" are less jealously barred, and only because they are connected with (substitutes or vehicles for) the infantile wishes. This apparent contradiction might be resolved in theory. But, for instance, Freud writes that "suppressed and forbidden wishes from childhood break through in the dream behind . . . unobjectionable wishes which are capable of entering consciousness," after insisting that the wishes first thought to be "represented as fulfilled" *were* in themselves objectionable and were *not* capable of entering consciousness.[44] Again, the wish-fulfillment-mind theory needs to postulate either the fulfillment of a special class of first-agency wishes or a particular kind of fulfillment, e.g., a too-direct one, in the case of distressing dreams. The postulate that they are distressing (to the second agency) because they satisfy wishes of the first agency will not do without elaboration, because (practically) all dreams are attributed primarily to the first agency and not all dreams are distressing. The postulate that the censorship of the second agency is directed primarily at infantile wishes—that it is these which it guards against and that its censorship of (unconscious) vehicle-thoughts or wishes, and the unpleasure it would find in their emergence, is less intense and only an extension of its censorship of and potential unpleasure in the infantile wishes—may be called in to fill the need. But then there is a conflict between this postulate and the previous insistence on the specific objectionability of all the "wishes represented as fulfilled" on first analysis—which are not leftover, infantile ones.

iii. Freud works out, in the transitional sixth chapter of *The Interpretation of Dreams,* the view of "dream-formation" ("dream-work") outlined above, which is almost strictly parallel to the quantity-level view of this part of the subject. But, if "a dream" is regarded as "representing" the "dream-thoughts" in the sense of consisting in some of them and pictorializing them—and on the other hand still as "representing a wish as fulfilled" in the sense of meaning (standing for) a proposition that fulfills a wish—these concepts have to be reconciled, but are not. More specifically, the transitional view of the dream as representing the dream-thoughts depends on the wish-fulfill-ment-mind view of the dream as representing a wish as fulfilled, but it becomes hard to say how a dream could be found to mean a proposition that satisfies or would satisfy a wish of the subject's if it is simply a pictorialization of the dream-thoughts (transference-thoughts) that have the greatest number of links with the rest.

D. Such difficulties are not what I am mainly concerned to point out. Freud used his previous theory, which applied to neurotic symptoms, as a basis for his new theories regarding dreams. But he used his new theories to cover dreams in order to get a bearing on the question of neurosis and neurotic symptoms, which was his and will be my central concern in the following chapters.

I regard the wish-fulfillment-mind level as Freud's strongest explicit theory, if Freudian theory is an instrument for describing, clarifying, correlating, and explaining Freud's material of observation. It was developed in closer connection with that material than the new quantity theory, was meant to be based on the material and its implications, and had less influence from the old framework and theory of affective ideas and quantity.

Conversely, I regard the new quantity theory as unrelated to the material of observation except through the wish-fulfillment-mind postulates or the considerations that Freud put forward in support of them, and not as supported by such considerations even if they did uphold the wish-fulfillment-mind postulates (just as, earlier, if the material had provided support for the postulate that the reason for and result of emotional reactions is discharge of affect that has become oppressive by reason of its excessive amount, it would not thereby have upheld the parallel postulate regarding cranial excitation); I regard the new quantity theory as demonstrably dictated by an expansion (and limitation) of the previous, misconceived quantity framework and theory, and as generating its hypotheses out of this framework and theory.

For these reasons, as I continue to develop Freud's third direction—his implicit theory of unconscious conflict—I shall be more concerned with the wish-fulfillment-mind version and its application to neurotic symptoms than with the quantity level.

4.   SYMPTOMS: PRELIMINARY INTERPRETATIONS

Freud's use of certain devices in place of hypnotism in such cases as that of Elisabeth von R. led him, in theory, to the "pathogenic material," specified as memories of traumatic events, which (or the strangulation of which, or the affect detached from which) was the cause of neurotic symptoms. In practice, by persuading a patient to recount in detail memories of events that took place about the time when his or her symptoms began, or grew worse, Freud got a *text* in which to discern, and demonstrate to the patient, an unconscious conflict from which the symptoms could (rather vaguely) be said to issue.

In theory, the technique of "free association" was another in the series for eliciting the "pathogenic material," now specified as, ultimately, unconscious infantile wishes, of which the "manifest" dream or neurotic symptom was the outcome and constituted the distorted substitution gratification. In practice, the "free associations" of the dreamer or neurotic to his own dream or symptom were again providing a *text* in order to come to a conclusion about the dreamer's or neurotic's state of mind.

In a mature case history, like that of the Rat Man, the developed text is much more complex than that of Elisabeth von R. In order to further develop the meaning of symptoms, and the kind of explanation Freud is offering, I shall make use of a device Freud used which I call the technique of provisional reports. Freud's use of it can be summed up like this: the subject's initial "associations" to some piece of behavior, say, led to a preliminary interpretation; then, perhaps at the same sitting, perhaps at the next, perhaps much later, further "associations" allowed the interpretation to be advanced a degree. At this point, the initial report was subject to review. It had to be seen as not the whole story, and it might be seen to have been in some respect misleading. Certain questions, too, that might have been asked but were unanswerable at the time of the first provisional report could be answered in the light of the second or third. And although Freud seldom thought he had reached the ultimate report in light of which all questions regarding a case could be answered, he did at least sometimes reach a point where a tolerably clear general picture was possible.

In what follows, the initial reports on Freud's explanation and on the validity of his theories in relation to his material will sometimes be immediately revised, and in any case will be seen retrospectively as only part of the story. Some of the questions that might be asked on a preliminary level will have to wait for elucidation until as many returns are in as are available. The provisional reports will be the means for developing a further picture, in light of which they can be revised.

1. RAT MAN: BEGINNING

In the case of the Rat Man, probably the clearest and most complete of Freud's few reports of a full psychoanalysis, appears the following example of the kind of activity Freud attempts to analyze: the Rat Man told Freud that, at a recent time, he had started a very severe course of diet and exercise in order to get rid of his fat (his *dick*). He had gone "tearing along the road without a hat in the blazing heat of an August sun,"[1] and panting up and down mountains. His weight-losing program was so violent that he could have seriously injured himself. The Rat Man was not obese; wearing himself out and making himself ill was unnecessary for losing some weight, even if he had been too fat. It was precisely in this respect that the behavior was, for Freud, "neurotic": there was an incongruity between the evident object, or the evident and stated intention, and the behavior. In the public world—that is, in the arena where we understand one another's actions by observing them, or by asking one another what we are doing or mean to do—there would be little to say about such behavior beyond "He is mistakenly trying to lose weight" or "He is trying to lose weight in a dangerous way." Some of the Rat Man's behavior was absurd in a rather more thoroughgoing way; it was "pointless" not just in being incongruous with its evident object or intention, but in having no discernible object or intention. For example, the group of thoughts and actions after which Freud gave the patient his pseudonym, in order to be understood, had first to be told over several times until the subject could be seen as having vacillated between several courses, which individually might have been evident, but if they had been evident, they would still have seemed incongruous.[2]

Freud's interpretation of a neurotic symptom or piece of behavior is placing it in the subject's private world, or finding out what it means to him that it would not mean to anyone else. He treats the evident behavior as primary text, or similar to "manifest content" of a dream, and the subject's "associations" as secondary text.

The Rat Man talked in connection with *dick* of the English cousin of the lady the Rat Man loved. His name was Richard. At the time of the patient's excessive reducing, he was visiting his cousin and taking up a great deal of her attention. In terms of this "association," Freud set up a first interpretation of the meaning that the patient's *dick,* and his behavior in regard to it, had for him:

> I try to get rid of my fat *(dick)*.
> *dick:* Richard
> I try to get rid of Dick.

But, looking back at the actual behavior in the light of this interpretation, it could not be ignored that the action was tending to get the Rat Man himself out of the way more than Richard. Freud said that the patient's behavior was "indirectly suicidal."[3]

2. SEEING-AS AND RESPONDING-TO

In the preliminary interpretation of the Rat Man's banting an important conclusion was that "he had been far more jealous of [Dick] and enraged with him than he could admit to himself."[4] His jealousy and rage at Dick were not, of course, evident in his behavior, and he did not proclaim them. What Freud reports of the Rat Man's talk about Dick suggests that, taken by itself, it would have led a listener to conclude that Richard, quite without meaning to, presented himself as something of a rival or inconvenience to the Rat Man's courtship; and that, reading between the patient's lines, one would have judged him more jealous of and angry at the supposed rival than he said or thought he was. But it was this talk as pursuant to his thinking of Dick in connection with his violent attempt to get rid of his fat that led Freud to the conclusion as to the extent of his jealousy and anger. It was as if his own behavior asked him the question, what is to be violently attacked and got rid of? and he answered, *dick*—Dick was taking up all her time. . . .

Conclusions of this sort are turned back to the "manifest" activity, in such a way as to resolve, by degrees, its apparent pointlessness.

Freud's interpretations—but not the formulas in which they are summed up—suggest that there is a similarity between the neurotic's view of some thing, person, situation, event, or the like (for instance the Rat Man's view of *dick*) and a fairly ordi-

85

nary kind of case in which the subject's view of a thing can be described as "seeing-as." For instance, one catches sight of a group of shadows at night, and gives a jump and a cry. Then—perhaps at once, perhaps later—one is able to say what one was experiencing the shadows as, what they were or meant to one for the moment; the jump and cry are not to be explained in terms of the shadows per se, but in terms of what one was seeing them as. I am not discussing cases of mistaking-for; of thinking, for instance, that a group of shadows is a grotesque face. But although there is no mistake (in the ordinary sense, at least) in cases of seeing-as, there may be a sort of conviction, as the subject's response may indicate. He would not say, afterwards, "I believed it was . . . ," but, perhaps, "I felt as if it were . . . ," or "it seemed to me as if. . . ."

One of Freud's examples: Little Hans saw a horse collapse in the street. Afterwards, he could not bring himself to go where he might possibly witness such an event again. Only later, in the course of psychotherapy, when the child provided "associations" to (or bearing on) the horse's collapse, was it possible to understand what it meant to him—or, to state the matter in accordance with the above examples, what he was seeing it as—and hence the reason for his avoidance of the outdoors.

The Rat Man's behavior begins to be explicable on the supposition that, as he thought later of Dick, who was in his way, in connection with his fat, which he tried violently to get rid of, he thought at the start of *dick* as Dick; or that, in certain respects, he was seeing his fat as his rival, and treating it accordingly in the sense that he endowed it with a quality that it might have had but did not, and that he had more reason to attribute to Richard, of being too much, in his way, to be got rid of; and that he directed toward it a hostility or a desire to eliminate that in itself it did not call for, but that he had some reason to feel toward Dick.

What the Rat Man expressed in his talk about Dick, and even more in connecting Dick with the *dick* that he violently tried to get rid of, was a jealousy and rage that he did not merely dislike, but that was far greater than he could admit to himself.

Freud's question is not how such an emotion would seem to others, but how it seemed to the subject. That the Rat Man wanted not to know of it was indicated by his lack of recognition of what he was doing when he viewed and acted in terms of it and by the indirectness and inexplicitness of his acting. But his opposition to it was measured not just by his unawareness of what he was doing, but also by the manner of his doing. He could see himself as attacking Dick—by way of what was close to destroying himself.

It would be hard not to see one's fat as part of oneself, or not to see such an activity as harming oneself. That the Rat Man saw it that way as he was performing it was indicated by his having come, during his exercising on the mountains, to a precipice, and having been for a moment on the "verge" of casting himself over.

A similar but less obscure episode in his life showed more clearly than this one why the patient was treating himself in such a way. While studying in the absence of his lady, who had gone to take care of her sick grandmother, the Rat Man suddenly felt commanded to cut his own throat, and had even gone to get a razor, when the counter-command occurred to him, "No, you must go and kill the old woman." Having become aware of this "obsessional impulse," he was prostrated with guilty horror.[5]

Freud's formulation "turning rage around on oneself" is of the sort that allows him to ascend from consideration of a jealous rage that one cannot admit to oneself to consideration of the vicissitudes of a quantity. (Such turning about is one of the things he held instincts could do, in the metapsychological paper on their "Vicissitudes.") As applied to the present instance, it covers—both indicates and obscures—that the Rat Man had a reason for treating himself as the one to be got out of the way; that is, as indeed Freud stated, he was extremely guilty over his rage—he was ready to punish himself for being so angry toward others. It covers, in the same way, the point that he wanted not to know of his rage toward others, and would sooner—literally—feel murderous rage at himself than at them.

In short, the Rat Man's expression of hostility toward Richard, in "associating" to his excessive exercising, allowed his behavior to be interpreted as a response to his fat seen as Dick in the respect of being in his way, to be attacked and got rid of, but more prominently as a response to himself as guilty and having to be punished for his jealous rage.

3. SUBSTITUTION

The old mobility theory that Freud developed in collaboration with Breuer was one of the obviously wrong-headed points in the strangulation–abreaction view of hysteria. It leaned evidently on quasi-neurological considerations; nevertheless, the examples that were used to illustrate it suggested a model of mobility that had no necessary connection with quantity, and it depended on this model for credibility.

Breuer, for instance, to illustrate the theory that any "motor innervation" of sufficient intensity and duration could take the place of any other for the central purpose of discharge, told the story about Bismarck: that, being angry at the king but unable or unwilling to show his anger, he relieved his feelings by smashing a valuable vase. The story makes sense, so it seems to support the explicit theory. But it would fit better in what is scarcely a theory: that in the grip of certain emotions, of which anger is sometimes a comedic example, a person who cannot or will not vent or satisfy his feelings on or in regard to their proper object may "take them out" on a substitute, and, if he has picked or hit upon a good one, may derive a measure of satisfaction from the deed. Bismarck, presumably, could not tell the king what he thought, and still less, as he might have liked to have done, smash him—either out of respect for the monarch or regard for his own position. Presumably, too, the vase was a good substitute, being in the first place not only breakable but, like the king, valuable, and in the second place something that he could ruin without the ill effects that would probably follow his acting directly on his anger, or, in Breuer's terms, resorting to the "adequate reaction."

The Bismarck type of case involves a response to or use of one thing as if it were another. It does not involve mistaking the substitute for the proper object, or even, quite, "seeing-as" or feeling as if the object at hand were the other, although part of what may make a substitute a good or satisfying one is its correspondence to the proper object, especially *as* an object: one takes something that can occupy one's hands or go in one's mouth if one wants a cigarette but is giving up smoking, and takes out anger, vexation, frustration, and so on, on things that are breakable, bitable, kickable, or otherwise hurtable.

Cases of Bismarckian mobility are examples of another variant on the theme of satisfaction besides those that have already been considered: in these cases, the subject neither literally gets what he (really, or primarily) wants, nor believes that he has obtained or done it, nor even, quite, feels as if he had it or had done it—but, in short, does something else instead that has a certain correlation with what he wants to do, or does what he wants to do in regard to some object, person, or what not, which corresponds in some respects—especially as an object— to the proper object of his desire, emotion, and hence action; and he derives some of the satisfaction he would have had if he had literally gotten or done what he wanted, had that been possible. And, where not doing the direct thing is owing to its danger or wrongness in the subject's view, or to his having for some reason foresworn it (rather than just to unfeasibility or the simple unavailability of the proper object), he has also the satisfaction of *not* doing that. One has something of (or something like) what he wanted, without the drawbacks of obtaining it. It is a way of having one's cake and not eating it too.

Freud's mature theory of "substitutive gratification" in neurotic symptoms can be taken as incorporating and centering around the model of mobility that was only implied in the examples used to illustrate and support his early quantity theory, with two additions; that is, it can be taken as asserting that a neurotic symptom is a satisfaction of the kind under consideration, but, primarily, of an unconscious wish (one of the infantile aspect of first agency), and secondarily, also of a "defensive impulse" of the Ego, second agency, or adult aspect. It is not immediately evident that the model of substitution is radically altered by the two additions that the "wish" considered primary, at least, is "unconscious," and that the subject's "substitutive" activity is "satisfying" two birds with one stone. And examples of neurotic symptoms and behavior can be summarized in such a way as to seem to fit the model.

But the model is radically altered by what the additions amount to in the details of particular cases; that is, when one considers in what sense, and why, something like the Rat Man's hostility toward his lady's cousin was "unconscious"— what sort of emotion it was, and how he regarded it—and when one considers in what way his behavior was, and was not, "satisfying" two birds at once.

The Rat Man's jealous rage was not the sort of thing (like Bismarck's anger at the king) that the subject can easily admit to himself and is not ashamed of, but for prudence's sake cannot express openly and directly; nor was it the sort of thing (like Freud's "megalomania"[6] or his patient's too constant love[7]) that one would prefer not to have, or know about, or for self-respect's sake express or act on openly or directly. If it had been like the latter emotions, the model might work, and could be expanded. The theory could be stated: the subject does something that gratifies, by means of a substitute, a desire or emotion that he would prefer not to recognize or display, thereby deriving something like or something of the satisfaction that he would have had in gratifying it directly, and also the satisfaction of *not* gratifying it directly, and he is enabled thereby not to become fully aware that he does want it or to demonstrate it to others. But the Rat Man's jealous rage was an emotion far greater than he could admit to himself; he did not just dislike or disapprove it in himself, but hated himself for having it to the extent that he had to punish himself severely for entertaining it.

To do something that indirectly satisfied an emotion or desire that one merely disliked or disapproved of could certainly be to do something that could be called a "satisfaction" without misleading; it could be a satisfaction for the subject. But an emotion or desire that one hates in oneself, that one is extremely guilty over, and that makes one think himself deserving of suicide could be fulfilled only in a way that could but misleadingly be called a "satisfaction"; to the extent that one did gratify such an emotion, he would be dissatisfying himself. Suppose that a man who loved his wife, and his own liberty, satisfied sudden anger against her by shooting her. There would be nothing paradoxical about saying that the action satisfied his anger; there is nothing paradoxical about saying that a person could satisfy a desire or emotion of his without himself being satisfied. But it would be misleading to describe such an action as a "satisfaction" without immediately qualifying that description by saying that it was, much more notably, a dissatisfaction for the subject. What may be said to be satisfied, almost or quite "in reality," is the counter to an emotion like the Rat Man's anger at a rival—for instance, his hatred or disgust at himself for being in a jealous rage. The Rat Man did not eliminate Richard, or do him the slightest harm. But through his substitute for Richard, he literally punished himself for his desire to eliminate him—and came rather close to eliminating himself. To satisfy such guilt and anger at oneself, even if it is called a "desire to punish oneself," is hardly a satisfaction to the subject.[8]

A person might take some satisfaction in doing a thing that meant to him acting on (without satisfying or fulfilling) a desire such as the Rat Man's to get rid of an interferer—if he were *capable* of being satisfied by such an activity. But whatever satisfaction the subject might take in such an activity if he could gain satisfaction from it must be cancelled, and not added to, by what is not just a secondary meaning of a neurotic symptom, but its actual tendency and real result: in the Rat

Man's instance, approaching the verge of the ultimate punishment of suicide.

But, furthermore, the neurotic does not seem to have the satisfaction of *not* doing what characterizes a case of Bismarckian mobility. The comparison above of an action that would "substitutively" satisfy an emotion or desire that is highly repugnant to a neurotic, such as comparing the Rat Man's jealous rage at Dick or the old woman to a man's shooting a loved wife, seems false; a truer analogy would be a case in which such a person, in his rage, shot an animal or pummelled a dummy instead. But to the extent to which *he felt as if he were* murdering his wife, the satisfaction of his anger would be a dissatisfaction to the man. And, even if it were not to him as if his wife were murdered, to the extent that he felt as if he were acting on a murderous rage toward her (though without consummating it), he would be dissatisfied.

The neurotic, in expressing a piece of behavior that can be called a symptom, is not in the position of one who breaks a vase or beats a dummy with the degree of awareness that one usually has in such cases that he is merely "taking out" his anger—that his substitute is only that. Neurotic "substitutive" action or responding-to—to anticipate a point that will be developed later—seems to involve a denial of or attempt to ignore an emotion-cluster or attitude that the subject cannot admit. It is as if the Rat Man were telling himself that he does not want to get Richard out of his way; what he wants to get rid of is his fat. But it also involves not just a treating-as, but a seeing-as, and this is a seeing-as that seems to involve a stronger or at least more prolonged feeling-as-if than is involved in most ordinary cases of seeing-as. For example, it seems weak, in view of Hans' response—his inability, for some time, to bring himself to go where he might possibly see a horse fall down in the street again—to say that he saw the event that he witnessed and feared as this or that, without adding that he strongly felt as if he had seen something far more fearful to him than the actual happening. A substitute object for the neurotic is not just a substitute, but what may be called an emotional equivalent of what he is seeing it as.

In the Bismarck sort of case, the subject, knowing quite well that (for instance) he is angry at the king, and that the vase is a substitute for the king, knows quite well that it is *only* a substitute. Thus he will not feel guilty or endangered in performing his substitutive response, as he would have felt in smashing or even making a verbal attack on the king; on the contrary, he has the satisfaction of *not* eating his cake (of venting his anger *harmlessly*), as well as the qualified satisfaction of having cake or venting rage at the king (or the unqualified satisfaction of his desire to smash something).

The neurotic, however, misses the satisfaction of acting harmlessly, which *depends* on the recognition of not doing what one must not do; or, to put it more positively, to the extent to which he feels as if he were acting on an emotion or desire that he regards as highly wrong and dangerous, he feels guilty and endangered, and the extent to which he does so seems to be great.

And a person like the Rat Man is unable to get the satisfaction of *not* doing but gets, instead, much of the dissatisfaction of doing, not only because he feels as if he does, but also, and mainly, because the emotions and desires that he opposes in himself seem to him so bad that he believes himself guilty just for harboring them. Consider the instance of the grandmother. The Rat Man's becoming aware of the "impulse" to kill her was enough to prostrate him with guilt even though he did not act on it, but against it in making a move to punish himself for harboring it.

The first interpretation of the Rat Man's banting left several factors unaccounted for.[9] There was not only the question why the subject considered the mere desire to attack or get rid of Dick, or its substitutive expression, so bad that he had to be punished for it, but also the question why he extended such a degree of hostility to Richard—who, after all, was not a serious rival, and whose interference with his courtship was slight, temporary, and unintentional.

These questions were answered through the further course of analysis by interpreting the Rat Man's attitude toward

Dick—his conception of him as an obstacle to his erotic gratification, his rage against him in this character, and desire to get rid of him—as directed properly to another person, the Rat Man's father, who, he believed, had meant to prevent his having any sexual satisfaction.

More than he was seeing his fat as Dick, he was seeing Dick as his father: his view of the lady's cousin was a view of The Interferer. His banting could thus be seen as directed ultimately at his father, and at himself in relation to his father; an attack on his fat, regarded as Richard, who was seen as his father, and an attempt to get rid of his fat or himself could be seen as being in a rage at Richard and wanting to get rid of him, and hence as being enraged at his father.

In terms of this (partial) interpretation, the unreasonable rage against not only Dick, but any person, such as the lady's grandmother, who was (however unwittingly) standing in the way of the Rat Man's erotic satisfaction, was accountable though in another sense still unreasonable; and so was his extreme guilt over it. To be in a murderous rage against anyone was horrible to him, but rage against his own father, to whom he had always been remarkably close and to whom he had always wanted to be a loving, obedient son, was much worse; he considered it monstrous.[10]

If the Rat Man had only been jealously enraged at Richard himself, or the old lady, one could perhaps imagine that his rage *might* have been the sort of thing that one only dislikes in oneself and would rather not have or act on, and could satisfy without entirely dissatisfying himself. To attack these people might have been something that he only did not want to be wanting.

The further interpretation showed why his rage against minor impediments was not like that: why he could not act on or express it in the most "substitutive" fashion, or even become vaguely aware of it, not acting on it, without having to punish himself severely and suffer a great sense of guilt as well. To attack his father, or get him out of his way, was something that, although he wanted it, he not only did not want to want:

he wanted it not to happen, and not only because he would be
terribly guilty if anything happened to his father through his
desire, but also because he believed he would be in danger of
severe punishment if he acted against him—and also because he
loved him. In other cases that are fully analyzed, neurotic
symptoms are also interpreted in terms of emotions or desires
that cannot be satisfied without entirely dissatisfying the subject, the fulfillment of which is something that he does not
want to come about even more than he wants it. In some cases,
the paramount reason for wanting the emotion *not* to be satisfied is that it implies a dreadful danger to the subject. For instance, Freud found a fundamental desire in the Wolf Man's
childhood neurosis to be his wanting to take his mother's place
as his father's sexual partner. But the boy believed that for this
desire to be satisfied, he would have to be castrated. Generally
there would seem to be both an implication of vileness or
monstrosity in oneself and an implication of horrible danger in
the prospect of the fulfillment of a fundamental, unconscious
emotion or desire. The two aspects of its great undesirability
may be combined in the conception of such a fulfillment as
entailing a punishment. Little Hans, for instance, wanted not
to act upon his rather jealous, erotically-tinged love for his
mother (a) because, as it was vaguely erotic, it seemed to him
to imply the danger of the fearful punishment he had been
threatened with for masturbating and (b) because, as it was
jealous, it implied a further desire to do some harm to his father—and for any harm to have come to his father would have
been a disaster for the boy.

4. "COMPROMISE-GRATIFICATION"

When people objected to the wish-fulfillment theory on the
ground that more people assess most of their dreams as unpleasant than as pleasant, and that neurotics as a rule do not
seem to find their symptoms pleasurable, Freud used to reply,

first, that one must consider not the "manifest content" of dream or symptom but its "latent content" before deciding whether it constitutes or provides a satisfaction, and second, that one must always ask, "Satisfying to whom?"—for what remains desirable and pleasing to the infantile aspect, Unconscious, first agency, Id, is no longer pleasing to the dominant, preconscious system, Ego, second agency, but is such as to call for unpleasure on its part.[11]

The view of the two agencies can be partially explained by the history of Freud's theory. It must be remembered that Freud began with a concept of "affective ideas" as entities within the psyche ("foreign bodies," which for a time he imagined that it was his therapeutic task to extirpate) or as units of ideational content plus quantities of excitation; even when he began to speak of "ideas" or "wishes" rather than of "affective ideas," much of his original conception remained. It showed up (a) in a pervasive assumption that "ideas" or "wishes"—especially those that fit into the developing theory as replacements for the original "pathogenic affective ideas"—could be regarded as independent of one another and almost independent of the subject, and as operating autonomously and automatically, according to laws of their own which had very little, if anything, to do with the conduct or thinking of persons and, for instance, having ends, strivings, and so on, other than those of the subject and (b) especially in his view of the unconscious, not greatly changed in his maturity from the repression-conversion view that the (neurotic) unconscious was that which the Ego, finding it antithetical, forcibly attempted to put aside or get rid of, and which, as a result of this attempt, became at once unconscious and pathogenic (split into an unconscious ideational content and a pathogenic quantity of affect or excitation, incapable of normal discharge but too great to be contained).

But one version of the two-agencies view mentioned in Chapter III might have been developed from or supported by some rather ordinary considerations.

We sometimes say that a person is behaving or thinking

"childishly," perhaps meaning that his behavior is "unreason-able," for example, against his own best interests, or badly thought out (since we suppose that in general adults are more reasonable than children); or that his thinking is "irrational"; or that his actions are violating standards of prudence, morality, or aesthetic discrimination that are thought of as characteris-tically adult (educated, civilized); or that he is acting on a desire or demand that is considered inappropriate in an adult. We might say, observing such behavior, that "A has a childish side," or that "A is satisfying the child in himself," or perhaps, "the child lives on in A." But what this means is that not A *contains* a child (or a childish body of wishes, or a childish as-pect) within himself, but that *he* is sometimes childish. It im-plies that he is sometimes not childish (if he never behaved like an adult, we would not say "he has a childish side"—or streak, or way of acting sometimes—but something like "he is just a child"); however, it does not imply that a part or aspect of himself is adult. If we talk about "the child living on in the adult," and so on, we mean the same sort of thing as when we talk about "behaving childishly." If there were any sense in saying something like "the core of his being is all infantile wishes" it would be to point out that "basically" or "at heart," the subject was just a child, or had never grown up, mentally or emotionally. If "A is satisfying the child in him," we might mean that he is satisfying a childish demand, or indulging him-self in a childish mood. And "behaving childishly" might be satisfying to the subject if he were in a childish mood; or one could "behave childishly" and not be satisfied (e.g., imme-diately regretting it because it was childish or for some other reason); or one could be at once rather pleased and rather dis-pleased (e.g., pleased in that he had what he childishly de-manded, but displeased in that he had made rather a fool of himself). But if A was "behaving childishly," and being at once rather pleased and rather displeased at the fulfillment of a "childish" demand, it was not that there was a childish part or aspect of himself that was being satisfied while the rest of him was being displeased.

Nevertheless, let me suppose that Freud's view of the two agencies—that there is an amoral, demanding, selfish, uncivilized, and in short childish side or self at the bottom or core of one's being, which is unable to think realistically or to plan for its, or the subject's, greater satisfactions, or to forgo immediate ones, which is all wishes, which wishes for and is capable of enjoying all sorts of things that are not desired by one's grown-up, civilized, realistic, self-respecting and self-preserving, prudent, moral, and aesthetically discriminating upper or outer self; things that would be unpleasing to the exterior side, and even shocking and disgusting to it—let me suppose that this view could somehow, literally, hypothetically, or metaphorically,[12] be used to clarify neurotic symptoms, and that Freud's view of symptoms as "compromise-gratifications," compromises between the two agencies, could, in some construction, be held. Consideration of Freud's specific interpretations demonstrates that his two agencies view is not a useful instrument for clarifying neurotic symptoms. In particular, the account of symptoms as "compromise-gratifications," on the one hand, and primarily, satisfying a wish belonging to the insurgent, childish interior—to the satisfaction of that aspect of the subject, but in such a manner that the wish-fulfillment is harmless, unreal, and unrecognizable, thus not dissatisfying the controlling, adult exterior—and secondarily also satisfying a "defensive impulse" of the adult side, to its satisfaction is not tenable, however it is construed.

Freud's investigation of neurosis does not reveal, on the one hand, repressed, unconscious, infantile wishes, and on the other hand, preconscious, adult "defensive impulses." So far, it appears that what is revealed, on any level of interpretation, are contrary dispositions or attitudes, which can be regarded as "emotion-clusters," and, for the sake of analysis, characterized as including factors of belief, emotion, and desire. For instance, the Rat Man's "associations" and, through them, his behavior may be said to have revealed, on one side of a conflict, a belief or conception (that his fat was too much, in his way, and to be eliminated; that Richard was the same; that his

98

father was interfering with his erotic satisfaction and was to be got out of the way), an emotion (hostility or murderous rage), and a desire (to eliminate); on the other side, the same sort of cluster: a belief that his hostility was monstrous and highly dangerous to himself and to his father; guilt and anger at himself; desire, need, or compulsion to punish himself, and desire not to entertain, express, act on, or know of his hostility.

Among the beliefs, desires, and emotions in terms of which Freud interprets neurotic symptoms, something like the Rat Man's murderous anger at his father/Richard/his fat and the beliefs and desires it involved come closer than anything else to the infantile wishes that are supposed to be gaining primary satisfaction in neurotic symptoms. At least, this attitude is what the subject most violently opposes and most vehemently wants not to "satisfy" or act on, know of, or entertain; if anything is "repressed," it is. And the fundamental attitude, e.g., the Rat Man's in regard to his father, "goes back," in some respect, to childhood; but so does his contrary attitude.

If Freud's view of the two agencies and of "compromise-gratification" can be taken as a metaphor, the metaphor fails, first of all, in the respect that the emotion or desire most nearly corresponding, in the neurotic's state of mind, to the repressed, infantile wishes of the theoretical account, which are supposed to gain the primary satisfaction in symptoms, is, for instance, an incestuous, homosexual love involving a desire for sexual satisfaction, when the subject believes that such satisfaction entails castration. Or the emotion may be a murderous rage against the subject's father, when he believes that its gratification would show him a monster, involve him in great danger, and rid him of a dearly loved parent. The subject may desire such a thing, but *he,* and not just his "higher self," *wants it not to come about.* It would not only be displeasing to his adult, prudent, moralizing side or self (or to him as adult, prudent, etc.) it would be a disaster to *him*. Not even his most infantile, selfish, imprudent side could take pleasure in this "grati-fication."

Such emotions and desires are not what is most promi-nently satisfied in neurotic symptoms; they are not satisfied, even in a minimal way. I argued before that to say that an emotion or desire is satisfied or fulfilled is to imply that it is consummated. The Rat Man may be said to have been acting, indirectly, on his rage against Richard, hence against his fa-ther in his character as the interferer, in his weight-losing pro-gram; his behavior was directed toward what would mean the satisfaction of this most repugnant emotion and the desire that it involved. But although the symptom, in part, meant for the Rat Man an attack on his father, by way of Richard, by way of his fat or himself, it cannot have meant for him that his father was eliminated—that his murderous rage was fulfilled. I mentioned before that in the incident of the grand-mother, the "impulse" to murder the interferer was not even indirectly acted on. Similarly, in Hans' case, the agoraphobia which was the only real symptom was not interpreted as meaning anything that would tend to satisfy the subject's most hateful, fearful emotions and desires, although the event that the symptom was preventing him from witnessing again was so interpreted.

A person might find some satisfaction in an activity that meant for him acting on, without fulfilling, an emotion or de-sire. But a neurotic is not capable of being satisfied by acting on the emotions or desires that he most fears and hates. Not the Rat Man's most childish, selfish, and imprudent side (or the Rat Man at his most childish) could take pleasure in an activity that meant for him acting on an emotion and desire that he regarded himself as deserving of death for merely enter-taining.

And although in a neurotic symptom the subject cannot be said even in a minimal way to be satisfying his most feared and hated emotions and desires, or to be obtaining any gratification from indirectly acting on them, he misses the satisfaction of not doing what he wants not to do, of acting on what he considers a very wrong and dangerous emotion *harmlessly,* or of acting on it in such a way as not to have become aware of it. Often it is to him as if he were acting on such emotions or desires (e.g., making an attack on his father), and it is clear that he does partially recognize them. His sense of guilt or anxiety, and his self-punishment or self-deprivation, are to be interpreted in terms of his hatred or fear of such emotions, or of himself for acting on or harboring them; one does not feel guilt over or punish oneself for an emotion that one regards as monstrous if one is quite unaware of it. Furthermore, the subject tacitly acknowledges his partial awareness of and repugnance toward such emotions. And even partial recognition is enough to plunge him into guilt or anxiety.

Freud said that the "latent content" of a symptom had to be considered before one could decide whether or not it was a satisfaction or "wish-fulfillment." This is correct: that is, neurotic symptoms can only be understood in terms of their meaning for the subject. But once they are so understood, their actual (though inexplicit) tendency or effect can be taken into consideration. It might be argued that if the Rat Man's reducing program did not mean the fulfillment of his murderous rage at his father, neither did it mean the fulfillment of his suicidal guilt and anger at himself. But, not to quibble about the meaning of "satisfaction," it is clear that the Rat Man came closer to satisfying his guilt and anger at himself than he did to satisfying the rage that he was angry at himself for having—if only because the attack on his father was very indirect, and its "substitute" object was himself: his father, of course, or Dick, was in no way harmed, but he was there, and he was harmed. His symptom not only meant, but was, a self-punishment. (Other symptoms, such as Hans' phobia, which will presently be considered in more detail, are not so much self-harmings as self-deprivations.) The most feared and hated emotions and desires are not satisfied: the opposition-emotions, such as guilt or self-hatred, nearly or partially are. It does not seem as if even one's most prudent, moral, self-respecting and self-protective side or self could be gratified in the satisfaction or near-satisfaction of such an emotion. It is not ordinarily, and it is not for Freud's subjects, a "satisfaction" to satisfy great guilt or anger at oneself except possibly in the desperate sense that a person might be slightly less guilty over harboring an emotion or desire that he regarded as monstrous if he punished himself for having it; but, as I pointed out, the Rat Man suffered from a sense of guilt as well as acting on it. It is misleading to call an activity that nearly or partially satisfies such an emotion a "satisfaction" unless one immediately adds the qualification that it is a dissatisfaction to the subject.

Neurotic symptoms, as Freud interprets them on preliminary and especially on further levels, are also obscured by being called "compromises." Certainly, they usually tend toward the indirect satisfaction of antithetical emotions and desires, and a single symptomatic action (inaction, pain, or whatever) may have antithetical meanings for the subject. In this respect the application of the term "compromise" to neurotic symptoms is clear enough. But to call them "compromises" implies, as indeed Freud held, that they are compromise satisfactions: that they conform to some model of action, choice, or the like in which a middle ground is found between the claims of rival parties at conflict, or between inconsistent desires, needs, goals, standards, or intentions of a person, so that each side has enough of what it demanded to satisfy it, more or less, without encroaching too far on the demands of the other side (without dissatisfying *it*).

I have been trying to show that neurotic symptoms, as Freud interprets them, do not conform to any such model. No side of the subject could be said to be satisfied in the satisfaction either of the emotions that he regards as fearful and loathsome— which he, not just his "higher self," wants not to satisfy—or of his opposing emotions, such as guilty anger at himself. Symptoms do not even mean the satisfaction of the most repugnant emotions, so that, even if the subject had a "lower self" that could be satisfied in their satisfaction, it would not be satisfied in a symptom; moreover, not one's lowest side could be satisfied in an activity that meant for him an action on an emotion that he considers himself deserving of suicide for entertaining. The most repugnant emotions, however, are usually acted upon in such a way that the subject has not the satisfaction of not-doing, or of acting harmlessly. In any case, he has not the negative satisfaction, or lack of dissatisfaction, of not-recognizing, for he is partially aware of the attitude that he would repudiate, and he suffers from guilt and anxiety as well as from self-punishment or self-deprivation—which, of course, is not a punishment or deprivation only to one side of him. Neither "side" has enough of what it demands for its satisfaction, or indeed anything of what it demands. On the side of an emotion like the Rat Man's hostility to his father, there is no satisfaction; but on the other side, there can be no satisfaction as long as there is a first side. That is, what the neurotic demands on the side of his opposition to something like the Rat Man's rage at his father, or the Wolf Man's erotic love of his father, is not that it be satisfied indirectly, nonliterally, harmlessly, and in such a way as not to be revealed to others, but that it be not harbored. Thus there *can be* no compromise.

There can be no compromise unless "compromise" is given a very peculiar application. Oddly enough, while holding in theory that a neurotic symptom satisfies a "wish" of the "first agency" to its satisfaction, and a "defensive impulse" of the "second agency" to the satisfaction of that part or aspect, Freud once compared the sort of "compromise" that a neurotic symptom may be to the sort exemplified in this story. The Parthian queen, believing that the Roman triumvir Crassus had "embarked on his expedition out of love for gold . . . ordered molten gold to be poured down his throat when he was dead: 'Now,' she said, 'you have what you wanted.'"[13] Hardly a compromise, since the satisfaction of the reprehensible love of gold is *cancelled,* not just modified, by its also constituting, quite a bit more prominently, the satisfaction of an opposing, punitive disposition. At least, however, in this case, the triumvir had his gold, which is more than can be said of the neurotic's "lower self," and the Queen presumably took satisfaction in the posthumous punishment ("gratification"), whereas the neurotic, on the side of his opposition to an emotion of his own, could be satisfied only by not harboring or not being aware of it, and has not this satisfaction or lack of dissatisfaction; and of course in punishing it he punishes himself.

The neurotic does not have his cake, but he suffers the ache of eating it just the same. Not, however, just the same. If it was terrible for the Rat Man to make an attack on his father (or even disobey him) by proxy or double proxy, doing not the least harm to anyone but himself, it would probably have been much worse for him to attack or even disobey his father outright. At least, in acting indirectly, inexplicitly, and covertly on an emotion that in his view is highly repugnant, frightening, and wicked—and in the same way on his opposition to it—he is not obliged to become fully aware of it. Elisabeth von R. was "shattered" and "cried aloud" when Freud drily put it to her that for a long time she had been in love with her brother-in-law. For the moment, she was in a worse state than when she had been "fending off" her awareness of her love and, probably, punishing herself for having it. The Rat Man's hostile attitude toward his father was, if anything, more thoroughly repugnant to him than Elisabeth's love to her.

It might be said that a neurotic symptom, though it tends toward the fulfillment of antithetical emotions or desires, is gratifying, or not dissatisfying, to the subject mainly in that it is not a direct action on, and does not oblige him to become fully aware of, what he wants, and wants not to want (feels, and wants not to feel); but this too, considering that he is well enough aware of what he most opposes in himself to suffer guilt or anxiety, and at the same time to have to punish or deprive himself, can scarcely be called "gratification."

This is a provisional report; a fuller account of what is revealed about neurotic subjects, in Freud's investigation, and of the interpretation of symptoms, will be provided later. But I think that the material that can be discussed at this point is sufficient to show that Freud's theoretical account of neurotic symptoms as "satisfactions"; as "compromise-gratifications";

as satisfactions, primarily, of unconscious wishes belonging to a first, infantile agency, and, secondarily, of "defensive impulses" belonging to a second, adult, preconscious agency; and as "compromise-formations," the joint work of two separate or distinct parts, aspects, systems, or agencies, is not tenable.

5. CONFLICT

Freud's case histories indicate that neurotic conflict can be partly summarized by saying that the subject has certain beliefs, desires, and emotions that he not only dislikes, but loathes and fears; or that he wants something that, even more vehemently, he wants not to come about. Again, such a conflict can be summarized by saying that a neurotic symptom is not a compromise, and that the subject's opposition to an attitude of his own is such that it admits no compromise. The case histories further show that the neurotic is in a conflict that can no more be solved by choosing one of the alternatives with which he seems to be confronted than by compromising between them, or between his contrary attitudes.

It seems to be characteristic of the neurotic to be unable to make up his mind in what appear to be quite ordinary circumstances of choice, to settle for one alternative and let the other go, or take whatever consequences there may be. Some instances from the case histories not only provide examples of this peculiarity but, by placing the situations in the subjects' private frames of reference, provide at once highly idiosyncratic explanations for each subject's vacillation or suspension and a general view of the reason why a neurotic is often unable to make a choice.

The Rat Man, for example, was once presented with a plan by his mother: he was to marry a rich and well-connected girl, with whose family his mother was associated; when he finished his professional training, her family's business would help him in his career. If he had followed this plan, he would have had to give up the woman he loved, who had no money.[14]

According to Freud, the Rat Man's response to this plan (upon which his mother was not at all insistent) was to "avoid the task" of choosing one or the other alternative by falling into a state in which he was unable to study, so to qualify himself in his position, and so to take any wife at all. In the public world, what he escaped was a choice between love on one hand, and money and social advantage on the other. Either alternative, one would suppose, would be preferable to neither and an uncomfortable state of suspended animation.

In itself, either course might have been acceptable. But the Rat Man *could* not choose one or the other, because of what the choice meant.

His father had opposed his possible marriage to the woman he loved; furthermore, he himself had once had to make a similar choice, and had given up a penniless girl for a woman who had some money—the Rat Man's mother. In terms of the subject's long-settled beliefs, which were clarified late in the course of the analysis—that his father was opposed to his having any sexual satisfaction, and that if he set himself up against his father in this respect, he would be putting himself in a position of dangerous and wicked hostility to him—the plan could be interpreted as signifying to him a choice between, on the one hand, renouncing sexual desires, and on the other hand, being a monster, while running the risk of punishment for himself and harm to his father. Even in his private view, the Rat Man escaped very little and gained nothing by his inability to settle on one course and let the other go, but his lack of decision between ceasing to have any sexual desire (which he seemed unfairly and arbitrarily commanded to do, and which he could hardly have done even if he had wanted to) and being in a position of wicked and dangerous hostility to his father (which was unthinkable) is comprehensible. Neither alternative was acceptable, or even possible.

In the situation after which Freud named the Rat Man, he

did not retreat from having to make up his mind, but spent several days in a desperate attempt to pursue two contradictory courses of action, one of which was manifestly impossible, being based on a mistaken direction from an army captain who struck him as cruel and told him of a sadistic torture.[15] The interpretation involved a complicated mass of material, and was never quite finished. But the core of the matter was that the subject saw himself as faced with a choice between obeying his father (which he had to do but could not) and disobeying him, with the implications as before. Whether he retreated into lassitude or tortured himself in an attempt to make up his mind, he was at stalemate with himself.

The same is true in cases in which there is no evident call on the neurotic to make a choice or to select one of alternative courses of action. For example, Hans might be said to have retreated, like the Rat Man from his mother's plan, into a state of suspended animation, but in the face of what was not apparently a choice situation: that is, his seeing the horse's collapse. In the course of treatment, Hans' notion that a horse might fall down, as the one he saw did, was interpreted as meaning that his father would be harmed through Hans' own jealous hostility. This on the one hand was what he wanted, in order to have his mother for himself; but it was also something that he emphatically wanted not to happen—partly because for any harm to have come to his father would have been a disaster for him.[16]

The event he saw could be regarded as meaning to Hans the possible results of his love for his mother and jealousy toward his father; it demonstrated or dramatized the possibility to the boy. It asked him, in effect, Is this what you want? He could not choose to face the consequences of his love for his mother, if these as he believed were his father's downfall and his own horrible punishment; yet, even if he wanted to, he could not stop loving his mother as he did.

In short, neurotic conflict is an emotional trap from which the subject cannot retreat, although he attempts to avoid it by retreating from or vacillating in the face of actual or possible situations. It is an emotional deadlock that he cannot resolve either by choice between alternatives or by compromise. The neurotic cannot compromise and he cannot be satisfied.

5. SYMPTOMS: PATTERNS OF THOUGHT

I have been trying to show that although the theory of wish-fulfillment-mind was, of Freud's explicit theories, the least bound up with and governed by the framework of particle and quantity, the most flexible, and, from the point of view of his material, the strongest, a preliminary look at his data in cases of neurosis, his way of approaching an explanation, and his particular interpretations makes clear that the strongest explicit theory was in certain central respects failing to account for his data, and providing a misleading view of his form of explanation. I have been trying to begin to show how Freud does in practice interpret cases of neurosis. In making these points, I have talked as if symptoms were fully understood (on preliminary and further levels) in isolation from the interpretation of all the various other activities—and reflections, memories, remarks, and so on—recovered in a case-history.

But this is not so, as in fact was suggested by showing that the comparatively comprehensible instance of the old woman was brought to bear on the first interpretation of the Rat Man's weight-losing episode—even the preliminary, first-level interpretation of a neurotic symptom is not accomplished in isolation from the interpretation of other behavior or thinking.

The nature of the deadlock in terms of which the Rat Man's weight-losing program, for example, was finally interpreted emerged from the preliminary interpretation of many and various activities, and the way in which these could be seen to go together. The point in question is not just one of procedure or method of investigation and treatment. To see how the final interpretation emerges from the comparison of many preliminary interpretations is not only to see an aspect of Freud's method of investigation that it would be easy to overlook, and that he never clearly formulated, even while demonstrating it in the case histories; it is also an essential step toward the further characterization of what Freud finds to be the neurotic state of mind, toward a more nearly final report on the meaning of neurotic symptoms and on the implicit theory, and toward a further demonstration that the wish-fulfillment theory fails to account for and explain Freud's data.

1. BEGINNING TO DELINEATE A PATTERN OF THOUGHT

In the first portion of the psychoanalysis of the Rat Man, the patient introduced a large amount of material, mostly concerning his relationships with other people, his thoughts past and present—including obsessions—and experiences and situations that seemed to him important.

Considering together the instances the Rat Man introduced, Freud began to find in them a pattern. The parts of the pattern were beliefs (or conceptions: e.g., a certain view of himself) and emotions. They began to form a pattern (a) by repetition and (b) by recurring in various arrangements or relationships in regard to one another, on the basis of which a possible structure relating all the parts could be seen.

For example, the subject told Freud:

A. He had tortured himself with guilt for a long time over not having been present when his father died. (This was not a matter to reproach himself so gravely for, especially since he had been specifically told that his father's illness would not come to a crisis that day.)[1]

B. In various instances, dating from his childhood to a time not long before his father's death, the Rat Man was troubled by "obsessive thoughts" to the effect that he would be more successful in his pursuit of some girl if his father were to die, or that he would prefer giving up hope of success with a woman to his father's death (as if these possibilities were alternatives). These thoughts arose in situations in which he conceived himself to be erotically frustrated. He felt very guilty over them.[2]

C. The Rat Man mentioned all at once that he and his father had been great friends "except on a few subjects"; that although he loved the lady, he had never had very strong sexual desires in regard to her; and that his sensual desires had altogether been much stronger in childhood than when he was grown.[3]

On the basis of point A and other instances in which the motifs of his father's death and a conviction of guilt were conjoined, Freud postulated that the Rat Man had something to reproach himself with more serious than his absence from his father's deathbed, but related in his mind to his father's death. These ingredients (father's death, guilt) recurred in point B— with the further ingredient of the subject's success with some girl or woman introduced in such a way as to seem to have been an alternative, in his mind, to his father's death. The idea that the Rat Man had something to reproach himself for (connected in his mind with his father's death), added to the parts "father's death" and "amatory success" as alternatives, suggested a provisional answer to the questions of point B: i.e., that the Rat Man had, in his "obsessional thoughts," been wishing his father would die (so as to have an erotic success). If he had desired his father's death, his conviction of guilt in both sets of instances was explicable. (If he had wished his father dead, he could have felt almost as if he were responsible for the event—although his only fault in deed was hardly "his fault.")

The relation of opposition already set up between regard for his father (his father's life) and erotic success provided a provisional answer to the question why the Rat Man mentioned in the same breath his friendship with his father "except on a few subjects" and his lack of erotic desire as an adult. His bringing together the two points in a breath, together with the opposition previously set up, suggested what the "few subjects" might be—i.e., sexual matters. This interpretation—or filling out—of the Rat Man's statement, together again with the provisional answers to points A and B, suggested that he believed his father to be opposed to his erotic gratification: to be "in some way or other an interference."[4]

Freud joined together the parts between which he was beginning to find relationships in these and many similar instances in a working hypothesis or rough sketch of the structure of the Rat Man's private world—a framework of beliefs (or conceptions) and emotions in terms of which he viewed events and situations, himself, and other people. Freud put it to the Rat Man that he considered his father to be in some way an obstacle to his erotic gratification, that he had been hostile toward him for that reason, and that he was guilty over his hostility.

When Freud communicated this possibility to the patient, he answered that he could not believe he had ever been at all hostile toward his father; but he promptly told a story of a woman who committed suicide when she realized that she wished her sister were dead, so that she could have her husband for herself. He said he felt as that woman did, and it would be only right if his thoughts were the death of him.[5]

2. FILLING OUT THE PATTERN

Much as, in the first portion of the treatment, the recurrence of emotions and beliefs in new apparent relationships tended to confirm the tentative conclusions that had already been reached as to relationships among them that were not so apparent, and

112

to point toward a possible structure in which all the recurrent parts might be articulated, there emerged from Freud's interpretations of various instances of the Rat Man's behavior and of his thoughts and memories, in the next part of the treatment, patterns of recurrence and arrangement that converged with those that had already been sketched out, and in terms of which Freud's hypothesis as to the structure of the Rat Man's private world was expanded and refined.

Again, a few examples:

A. There were several instances, including that of Dick, that Freud interpreted in terms of the subject's hostility toward some person who might be considered to be interfering with his pursuit of a woman or erotic activity, and of self-punishment, which seemed a response or reaction to his hostility. The pattern of arrangement in the instance of Dick—the Rat Man sees a person who is in fact a slight and unwitting obstacle to his courtship as a serious rival, is jealous and enraged with him, and has to punish himself for his anger—is repeated in the instance of the grandmother.6 Then there was a series of instances that, in interpretation, constituted a variation on the last arrangement: they were analyzed as tending to protect himself and others from the effects of his rage. For example, he removed a stone from a road the lady was soon to travel—but then he put it back. The lady herself fell into the category of obstacles at the time of this incident, because she had been cold to him.7

B. Freud settled upon the patient's mother's plan to marry him off to a rich woman as the "exciting cause" of his becoming severely ill; he interpreted the event as signifying to the Rat Man a choice between satisfying his erotic desires and following his father's example and desires.8

C. The Rat Man mentioned that he had masturbated (or indulged in any sexual activity) very little since his early childhood; after his father's death, he masturbated more for a time, but felt very guilty about it, and dropped it again, and that since that period he had masturbated only on certain special occasions. He did not know why he should have done it then; the circumstances struck him simply as inspiring. He mentioned two: hearing a horn blown very beautifully in the middle of Vienna—something rare, because there was a regulation against it—and reading a moving story in which a man whose dead mistress had put a curse on any future lover of his had at last been able to break through his fear, and kissed his new love joyfully. Freud noted that the occasions had something in common besides being inspiring: "a prohibition and the defiance of a command."[9]

The constant repetition in the Rat Man's thoughts, in his memories of events and situations, in his own obsessions from his childhood until the present time, and in the interpretation of his behavior, of certain motifs—his father and his father's death, his sexual gratification or frustration, the interference of some person with his sexual activity, rage, fear of rage and guilt—indicated that these ingredients were focal points in the Rat Man's world: that is, he was concerned with them to the exclusion of other considerations, and he tended to conceive of and respond to all situations, events, and persons in terms of these elements. The repetition of these focal points in various arrangements began to indicate that they fell together in a larger constellation than what any one instance had provided: that they were related together in a consistent conceptual-emotional framework.

Freud's final hypothesis, which he put to the Rat Man, was that the patient had, as a child, considered that his father stood in the way of his sexual activity—probably masturbating—that he had therefore been angry with his father, and perhaps that he had stopped masturbating upon his father's insistence or punishment.

3. CHILDHOOD MEMORY: STRUCTURE OF THOUGHT

The Rat Man responded to Freud's "construction" by telling him a story his parents had often told him, of an event in his childhood. His father had beaten him very severely; the family story had it that he was punished for biting, but in the patient's fantasies, at least, the crime was sexual. He flew into a rage with his father so violent that both of them were greatly shaken. He said that after the event he became a "coward," and that his father never beat him again.[10]

The Rat Man's report of his last beating provided a key to what had gone before in the course of his analysis; it brought together, in a single constellation, the beliefs, emotions, and desires that severally figured in the interpretation of various thoughts, symptoms, and pieces of behavior, and it presented these motifs as related together in a theme, with which the relations already posited among them were consistent. In the Rat Man's fantasy-memory, that is, his father was strongly opposed to his masturbating; he forbade and punished it. (Therefore to engage in such activity would be to disobey his father.) In the Rat Man's memory, he was enraged with his father in his role as obstacle and punisher, but was frightened at the extent of his own rage. (The possible results of his anger were to be feared. Both—though this was vague in the memory—what he might do in anger and further punishment were to be feared.) If to this arrangement of ingredients was added the Rat Man's very great affection for his father and desire to please him and conform to his desires, which had been explicit and implicit from the beginning, then it provided an overall pattern or blueprint in terms of which, for instance, the opposition already posited in the subject's mind between his love and obedience to his father and his erotic desires could be seen as related to his finding the blowing of a horn in the middle of Vienna an inspiration to masturbate; and this again as related to the thought that occurred to the Rat Man on the first, and one of the few occasions when he experienced coitus: "This is glorious! One might murder one's father for this!"[11]

Freud used the memory in an attempt to prove to the patient the central point that all along he had refused to believe, even when he seemed tacitly to assume it—that for a long time his love and desire to obey his father had been in conflict with a serious hostility toward him. A part of the function in therapy of such a memory is similar to that which the memories of

115

"traumatic events" had in the early cases, such as that of Elisabeth von R.: it is a text in which to discover an unconscious conflict, and with which to demonstrate its existence to the patient.

Freud sometimes considered such events as the Rat Man's last beating—that is, the events that the subject remembered, falsely remembered, or partly remembered and partly fantasized as having occurred in his childhood, which had a key position in Freud's investigation and treatment—as "causes" of neurosis. His explicit theory had it that childhood events could constitute underlying or predisposing causes of neurosis (a) as bringing about or leading to fixation and (b) as bringing about or being the occasion of repression.

There are two questions here: whether such an event (truly or falsely remembered) as the Rat Man's last beating can in any sense be considered an underlying cause of neurosis or of the conflict at its core; and what relation there is between the explicit (libido) theory as it bears on the underlying causes of neurosis and the childhood events, or fantasies, which Freud does treat as important in psychoanalysis, and what application this part of the theory has to Freud's cases as he reports and interprets them.

According to the libido theory, fixation is the persisting attachment of a quantity of libido to a component of the sexual instinct, or to a pregenital organization or Oedipal object, or to an infantile path to satisfaction, etc., and comes about through (experiences comprising or leading to) the excessive or premature stimulation or satisfaction of the component-impulse (etc.), in conjunction with the subject's innate libidinal constitution. The underlying causes of obsessional neurosis are in theory fixation at, upon, or of, and repression of the anal-sadistic component or organization of the sexual instinct.[12]

The case history of the Rat Man, and Freud's other case histories, at least show that the explicit theory of underlying causes (fixation and repression of, or "at the point of," pregenital organization or component-instinct) has—however the "instincts" and "fixation" and "repression" are construed—no central and no evident place in cases of neurosis as Freud investigated and treated them, and that his cases of neurosis are not elucidated in terms of the sexual instinct and its components.[13]

Freud considered and treated the Rat Man's childhood memory as important because it illustrated, as comprehensibly related to one another, a structure of conflicting beliefs, emotions, and desires toward which the interpretation of the material previously considered had been tending—and in terms of which that material could be further interpreted. The event (however in fact it occurred) obviously cannot be supposed to have occasioned the fixation or the repression of the anal–sadistic component, organization, or inclination (however repression and fixation are defined), nor can any other events mentioned in the report. The memory illustrated the conflicting beliefs, emotions, and desires in terms of which the subject's symptoms, and other material, were interpreted.[14] The memory did not illustrate the sadistic-anal component, and the conflict in terms of which symptoms were interpreted was not between the sadistic-anal impulse and defenses against or opposition to it (or a clash between libido seeking discharge by infantile "paths," or desires or inclinations that characterize a pregenital organization, or fit under the head of a component-instinct, and the Ego or defense impulses). Where can anal-sadism come in?

In the discussion of obsessional neurosis that follows the case history proper of the Rat Man, Freud can be seen at work applying his instinct-categories to the material at hand, seeking to account for the subject's conceptual-emotional conflict by placing one of its ingredients under the heading of a component-instinct. He first generalizes the conflict into one between love and hate, and then tentatively places hate under the heading of sadism.

But in this discussion he acknowledges, in effect, that if hatred or hostility is to be accounted for in terms of the instinct-groupings, it must be found not just to belong in the very broad general category of negative emotions, desires, and

117

tendencies (including aggressiveness, unkindness, anger, cruelty, irritation, dislike, and so on) but either to be distinctly "sadistic"—that is, to be in the nature of cruelty, sensual or semisensual subjection of the object to oneself, or perhaps a twisting of love into hatred, or a relation to another person in which an underlying tenderness is expressed in harmful or hateful acts or desires[15]—or to belong in a developmental series with infantile sadism (in which, to accept Freud's grouping, sensual pleasure in cruel activities is closely related to teasing, balking, and other forms of resistance and attempts to subject others to one's will, and hence to anal aims—non-elimination, smearing, and so on).

The only point in the Rat Man's case history that seems at all to lend support to a view that his hostility to his father belonged in a series in which infantile anal-sadism was the beginning was that the patient had had an interest in elimination and allied matters as a child which, Freud thought, may have been prolonged by infestation with worms.[16] Freud, despite his theory, stated in the concluding discussion of obsessional neurosis that although he suspected some connection between infantile sadism and the extreme hatred or hostility that could (broadly speaking) be said to be in conflict with love in the Rat Man's and other cases—not, he noted, only cases of obsessional neurosis, but also of other neurotic illnesses that he had not attributed to the fixation and repression of infantile sadism—he could not demonstrate any connection, and what the relationship might be "remains completely obscure."[17]

There was no reason to think that the Rat Man's hostility to his father was itself a variant or eruption of sadism. It was in one sense the other side of love for the same person, but it was not love gone wrong or exhibited as hatefulness; rather, the subject both hated and loved his father, for what were to him reasons, that is, according to beliefs. The memory confirmed what Freud had postulated, that the Rat Man's rage against his father was in accordance with his beliefs that his father was opposed to and would punish his sexual activity and that to indulge in it would be to disobey his father. In his view, at

118

least, there was some reason for his hostility toward his father; it has not to be accounted for in terms of his instinctual makeup.

In one instance, sadism (and "anal" forms of expression) did enter the Rat Man's case, but in this instance it was not that his fundamental hostility could be considered a variant or eruption of sadism, or in a series with infantile- and anal-sadism, but rather that it erupted as sadism. In the Rat Man's encounter with the cruel captain, who at their first meeting told him a story about a form of torture involving anal penetration by rats, the subject's initial response was interpreted later as having included a feeling that the captain ought to be punished in the same way, and an obsessive fear that the torture might happen to the people he loved. In his voluminous "associations" to the incident, there was a great deal of "anal" detail. But, while the whole matter gives some indication of Freud's reasons for grouping the anal with the sadistic, and while it is clear that *the captain* was something of a sadist, it is not clear that the Rat Man was more than commonly sadistic or "anal" in desire or tendency, or—what the theory, however construed, requires— that (anal) sadistic tendencies or desires were what he "repressed." His view of the captain was again a view of his (punishing, interfering) father; his concomitant hostility, given this immediate object, naturally enough took the form "it should happen to you." His "not wanting to know" did not concern the "anal-sadistic" content that happened to be present, but rather concerned the central conflict: that is, he wanted not to recognize his hostile response as such.[18]

In short, although the Rat Man was not devoid of tendencies and modes of expression that could be designated "anal" or "sadistic," these tendencies and modes of expression were not in themselves central in the interpretation of his neurosis; Freud gave no indication either that he was more than commonly endowed with them, or that he had "repressed," or resisted becoming aware of them, except as they were (accidentally) related to his central conflict. Freud did not show that the Rat Man's hostility to his father was a descendant of infantile sa-

119

dism, or otherwise fitting under the heading of sadism, but rather indicated that it was not. It seems to me that the main objection to Freud's instinct-categories is his tendency to use them seemingly to account for a desire or emotion, while in fact only placing it under a general heading—which may obscure its particular character. A rather different example from that in the present case of what I take to be a misleading use of the instinct categories (seemingly accounting for a desire, emotion, tendency, or attitude) is Freud's assertion, on the basis of analyses of some dream-meaning-construction of his own, that the trait of ambition can be traced to (develops in sequence from) infantile urethral erotism, or difficulties in urination. It seems to me that what Freud's dream-constructions demonstrate is that some children may express what is already ambition (or "rebellion," or "megalomania") through conspicuous urination (and suffer blows to their self-regard in consequence)—as when Freud, a little boy, relieved himself in his parents' room, and in their presence—and/or express a certain ambition or self-exaltation in connection with "difficulties in micturition"—as when still younger Freud, reproached for wetting his bed, promised to buy his father a nice new red bed in the town of N———; and that, in one case at least, memories of such events remained central to the subject, as summing up the polarity between high and low estimation of himself, in relation to others (first, in relation to his parents). If this is right, then (a) the assertion as to sequential relationship is incorrect, (b) the placing under an "instinct" heading obscures, rather than clarifies, the character of the emotions, desires, or attitudes in question, (c) it obscures a relation between childhood emotions and desires and adult ones, which is (here) at least clearly suggested by the details of the material—not the placing under a heading, and (d) it obscures the character of central memories of childhood and the relation they have to an adult's pattern of thinking.[19]

But, furthermore, what the memory illustrated (and what the symptoms were interpreted in terms of) was not just the putative derivative of sadism—hatred or rage. Although Freud said (again in the semitheoretical concluding discussion) that "We may regard the repression of [the Rat Man's] infantile hatred of his father as the event that brought his whole subsequent career under the dominion of the neurosis,"[20] the patient's memory-fantasy illustrated a structure of conflicting beliefs and emotions, all closely related to one another. The beliefs and emotions tending to oppose his hostility to his father (beliefs that his rage was dangerous to himself and to his father, fear and guilt, love of his father and desire to obey him) could scarcely be separated from that emotion and the beliefs upon which it rested; they were a structure, or parts of one attitude. And, although the Rat Man's general love for his father and desire to be a good son to him were more or less explicit, otherwise the entire structure illustrated in the childhood memory was unconscious in the same sense that the rage was. What was demonstrated in the memory was not just the subject's "infantile hatred," but a conflict of which the hatred was a part.[21] Again, it was the conflict in terms of which symptoms and other phenomena were being interpreted. If Freud was to account for the patient's neurosis in terms of fixation and repression—or in terms of the presence and unconsciousness of some mental state—he had to account for the presence and unconsciousness of an entire structure of conflicting beliefs and emotions. And the Rat Man's last beating does not look any more promising as the occasion of fixation or repression of the subject's rage or hostility toward his father than as the occasion of the fixation or repression of the remainder of the beliefs and emotions that the memory-fantasy illustrates, however these terms, central to the theory but never clearly defined, are accepted.[22]

If a specific event or experience could account for the subject's having, or his being unconscious of, beliefs, emotions, and desires, the likeliest relation between the event and the beliefs and emotions would seem to be that the event served to persuade him of them or convince him of their appropriateness, or to persuade him that he must not have them or express or act upon them, so that he would try afterwards to be unaware of them.

It is highly unlikely that the Rat Man's last beating, supposing that it occurred just as he remembered, and in accordance with the fantasies that he built up around it, in itself could have persuaded him either that his father was opposed to and would punish any erotic activity of his, that his anger at his father for interfering and punishing was wrong and dangerous to himself and his father, or that he must not harbor the beliefs and emotions in question.[23] It seems probable that there were other events and influences in his situation as a child that combined with his last beating to persuade him that his father was much opposed to his sexual activity and would prevent or punish it, to arouse his anger against his father in this role, to make him believe that his own anger was to be feared, and so on. Supposing his version of the event to be partly a product of fantasy—supposing, for instance, that his mother was right in believing that on the occasion when he frightened himself and his father by falling into an extreme rage, he was being punished for some nonsexual misdemeanor—it remains likely that other events, suggestions, hints, threats, and the like that preceded (and some of which may have followed) the beating combined to impress the beliefs and emotions on him, and to teach him to want not to know them.

Yet these particular conflicting emotions and beliefs could not be clearly attributed even to the sum of the subject's childhood experiences or the training his parents, perhaps unwittingly, gave him, so far as these were known: Freud had no evidence that anything in the subject's experience was such as to make it very likely that he would hold this set of beliefs and emotions.[24]

Neither the beginning nor the unconscious character of a neurotic conflict (or the beliefs and emotions that make it up) can convincingly be attributed to a single event or experience, or to a number of specific events; its presence cannot even with any certainty be attributed to the general character of the subject's experience, so far as it is discovered in psychoanalysis.

But, granted that what Freud was finding out was a structure of conflicting beliefs and emotions, and not a fixated and repressed infantile wish or component-impulse, it should not be surprising that he was unable to account for it in terms either of the subject's makeup, sexual or otherwise, so far as it could be discovered, or of specific events or experiences in his childhood, so far as these could be reconstructed. The neurotic state of mind differs in several respects from what one assumes, at any rate, is a nonneurotic set of beliefs and emotions. But it does not differ in any respect that makes it, as against for example a persistent and rigid set of beliefs or preconceptions in a nonneurotic, capable of being traced to a specific source or datable in its inception or in its being explicit, implicit, proclaimed, or denied.[25]

Some critics[26] seem to think (as indeed Freud himself thought when he first discovered that many of his patients' childhood "memories" were fantasies) that if such events as the Rat Man's last beating are in an unsure position between fact and fiction, and thus—if for no other reason—at least highly questionable as underlying causes of neurosis, then they are of no importance in the patient's condition or its investigation, and Freud's explanation loses much of its value. They are depending on the assumption that Freud's investigation is aimed at discovering the causes, or at least the genesis, of neurosis. But Freud's investigation, as distinguished from his explicit theory, is not aimed at discovering the causes of neurosis. If it had been, Freud might at least have made greater efforts than he did to discover exactly what did occur in the subject's childhood, and, for example, to check his memories against other evidence. In fact, where there was evidence counting against the factual correctness of the subject's version of his childhood experiences, Freud did not ignore it, but he continued to treat the subject's version as of primary significance.[27]

The justification for this procedure is clear in the context provided by a case history: what was being discovered was the subject's state of mind or structure of thought. Freud could find out through childhood memories—whether much or little overlaid by fantasy—a good deal about what the subject thought was of importance in his childhood, and even more about a pattern of belief and emotion underlying not only his neurotic symptoms but much of his thinking, behavior, and way of viewing "reality." Freud was demonstrating the presence of such a pattern of thought, not its inception.

It seems a probable conception of the place his father's beating (his memory of the event, or of being told about it) had in the Rat Man's mind that it was the center and epitome of a constellation of beliefs and emotions for him; it gelled them, so to speak, and it undoubtedly served as the core of "an imaginative production of positively epic character"[28] that he built up around it as a child and/or as an adolescent. Such a memory or pseudo-memory may give some indication of the general character of the subject's childhood, as he saw and sees it; it may be his way of remembering what, in his view, influenced his central, unconscious beliefs and emotions. It may serve him as a myth of origin, being an illustration at once of his view of the persons and events that most impressed him as a child and of his primary beliefs and emotions. (What happened to me, and what I thought and felt, is summed up in this story.)

Within the context of the previous course of Freud's investigation, such a memory or pseudo-memory served, as I said, to show in what structure the beliefs and emotions that were already being found to be constantly recurring in the subject's thinking and behavior were related to one another, and to demonstrate to the subject what his central, unconscious beliefs, emotions, and desires were.

Whether or not the *event* could be considered a cause, source, or influence is a red-herring question. In any case, that constellation or framework of beliefs, emotions, and desires that was elucidated in the Rat Man's memory was primary, in the sense that it was what Freud's interpretation of all the various instances of the Rat Man's thinking and behavior had been tending toward; neither any larger structure, nor any prior or simpler beliefs and desires were forthcoming or necessary to account for this constellation.[29] And from the opposite point of view—that is, starting from the patient's recollection of such an event, and considering the conduct, thinking, and feeling that occurred later in his life (though much of it was considered earlier in the analysis)—the emotional-conceptual structure embodied in the childhood memory is also seen as primary. In terms of the Rat Man's recollection, not only are Freud's hypotheses about his relationship to his father and the way he considered erotic satisfaction as a boy and a young man confirmed, but the peculiarities therein are seen as falling into place in a pattern of beliefs, emotions, and desires that apparently was established early in his life.[30] The elucidation of this pattern is turned back on the instances that had already been interpreted to the first level: the pattern can be seen as asserting itself in situations that had no evident relation to the primary one—for instance, it could be seen in the Rat Man's behavior toward his own *dick,* his obsessive thoughts concerning the lady's old grandmother, and his excessive protectiveness, on certain occasions, toward the lady herself. In these instances, the Rat Man could be seen as conceiving of some person as an equivalent to his father in his role of obstacle, feeling toward him, as such, a blind rage, and conceiving of his own hostility as guilty, punishable, and to be averted. Only in terms of this further interpretation could, for instance, his attitude toward Dick, and his great guilt in these instances, be explained.

The interpretation, in terms of the basic structure of thought and emotion, of behavior and thinking that occurs later in time than the recollection of childhood events may be of greater therapeutic importance than the turning back on behavior previously analyzed. The Rat Man, for instance, although he produced the often-told story of his last beating and the series of fantasies that he had built around it, and although he attributed his "cowardice" to the event, still refused to believe either that it had actually occurred or, what Freud had hoped to convince him by it, that he had considered his beloved father with hostility until the same group of beliefs, emotions, and desires appeared in yet another incarnation, in his relation to the therapist.

For instance, the patient would heap abuse on Freud—though apologizing all the time, and berating himself as a worthless wretch—and developed the habit of getting up and walking about while he abused Freud. He accounted for this habit by his delicacy of feeling, but finally he was convinced that it was the expression, rather, of a fear of getting a blow, and that the whole of this conduct, including the abuse, was unwarranted by anything in the present situation; he had "transferred" to the analyst the beliefs and emotions that applied to his father.[31] (It may be noted that the therapist's behavior in such a phase of "the painful road of transference"[32] is calculated not only to convince the patient that he is treating the doctor as a "substitute," and hence to make him aware of the inner deadlock he is imposing on the situation, but also, like Freud's early ways of "melting resistance," to help the patient come to terms with himself. Simply allowing the patient to "act out" such a conflict, within the therapeutic context, seems to be directed to both ends, and the analyst's continued expression of kindness and respect especially toward the latter one.)

In sum, the picture that emerges from Freud's reports of psychoanalytic treatments is this: what is finally indicated in the neurotic subject is a pattern or structure of conflicting beliefs, emotions, and desires. On the one hand, it is a constellation, or fixed grouping, of beliefs and emotions that—as a whole—seems to go back to childhood. The beliefs and emotions are in regard to the subject's situation as a child—as it seemed to him—and to people who were of great importance in his childhood and his relation to them; some of his memories of events that happened in his childhood (together with others regarding his thoughts and behavior as a child, such as the Rat Man's obsessional thoughts regarding his father and his amatory success, which began at an early age) at least suggests that he conceived this set of fundamental beliefs and emotions as a child. On the other hand, the fundamental structure of thought and emotion is a framework or blueprint that the subject must be considered more or less continuously to be imposing on the people, events, and situations that he encounters later in life. The neurotic's private world, that is, his way of viewing the aspects of "reality" that he meets, is understood in terms of the structure of thought and feeling that emerges gradually in the course of therapy. The mass of memories, symptoms, and other behavior, thoughts, assessments of himself and others, dream-reports, and so on that he supplies, and their first interpretation through "associations," leads to the understanding of the pattern in his seeing things and responding to them. His symptoms as an adult neurotic (and "transference" behavior, and so on) are fully interpreted in terms of the primary pattern.[33]

Freud remarks that a neurotic is "marooned in the past"; he may, like the Rat Man, be expressly concerned with the persons and situations that were important to him in childhood. In every case he is seen to be viewing elements in his latter-day circumstances as equivalent to the early persons and situations, and as constantly meeting in new guises an old emotional conflict.

According to this picture, the neurotic's pattern of thinking and feeling is unvarying and rigid, in the sense that the whole web of emotions and conceptions is constantly being activated. The Rat Man, for instance, is continuously finding himself in situations in which he considers himself to be sexually frustrated; he cannot consider himself frustrated without feeling as if some other person were to blame, and being angry at that person, but he cannot express his anger (however indirectly) or become aware of it (however vaguely) without feeling guilty and punishable. Again, he cannot allow himself any erotic satisfaction without feeling at least recklessly disobedient, and often also as if he were doing his father harm—"One might murder one's father for this!" He seems, in fact, to have come to view practically every situation and every person he encounters through the goggles of the old conflict. The pattern seems unvarying and rigid in the strange sense that it remains in operation when, one would think, the beliefs should have been overcome, the desires should have been abandoned: the Rat

Man remained torn between his erotic desires and his desires to obey his father and not to retaliate against his father's punishment, when he was a grown man, no longer subject to his father's authority; when his father would probably not have objected to his obtaining sexual satisfaction (though he did oppose the patient's pursuit of his lady); and when—as Freud was at first amazed to discover—his father had been dead for a matter of ten years.

6.   WANTING NOT TO KNOW

Invitis occurrit, do what they may, they cannot be rid of it; against their wills they must think of it a thousand times over; *perpetuo molestantur, nec oblivisci possunt,* they are continually troubled with it, in company; out of company, at meat, at exercise, at all times and places; *non desinunt ea quae minime volunt cogitare;* if it to be offensive especially, they cannot forget it; they may not rest or sleep for it, but still tormenting themselves. (Robert Burton, *Anatomy of Melancholy*)

Freud held in theory that the leftover, infantile, "unconscious wishes" ("the core of our being") are "indestructible."[1] The full interpretations of neurotics, viewed in the contexts in which they are reached, show not only that desires are persistent, but that in neurotics a conflicting structure of thought is "unconscious" and seems to persist from childhood. They show that whatever desires are involved are not only not all that is involved, and not only not satisfied in neurotic symptoms, they are also less the heads of the family, so to speak, than the element of belief. That is, a neurotic's symptoms and all sorts of activities, thoughts, and so on are understood as his responses to some thing, person, or situation as he sees or conceives of it, and he conceives of it in terms of old attitudes, of which again beliefs are the heads. If the Rat Man had not viewed Richard as an embodiment of his father, in his role of interferer, he would not have been enraged at him or wanted to get rid of him; if he had not believed that his father was forbidding and punishing his erotic satisfaction, he would not have been hostile to his father.

The neurotic, like anyone possessed of a firm set of beliefs, prejudices, or preconceptions, though "unconsciously," sees events, people, and the situations in which he finds himself as illustrating, realizing, or substantiating his beliefs. What is remarkable about the neurotic is not only the persistence or "indestructibility" of his fundamental beliefs and emotions, but the rigidity and narrowness of his structure of thought, and the constancy of its operation.

The first interpretations of all kinds of instances—almost everything the neurotic subject brings up for consideration and analysis—come together in such a way as to show more and more clearly that the subject has a fixed pattern of belief and emotion, which he is constantly imposing as a sort of blueprint on his experience. The Rat Man, for instance, had to be seen to be viewing the most various situations as representations of the situation of his childhood as he remembered it: he was very often seeing himself as frustrated in love, fixing on some person as to blame for his frustration or interfering with his satisfaction, and so on. Not everything the neurotic presents for consideration is a neurotic symptom, but most of what he shows or mentions—memories, reflections, remarks about himself and others, behavior in relation to the therapist and other behavior aberrant and not so aberrant, instances of inactivity or inability to act, dreams—leads to the formulation of his fundamental structure of conflicting beliefs and emotions, and can in the end be understood as symptomatic of it. The subject may quite early in the course of psychoanalysis be found to be preoccupied with certain themes, to the exclusion of other concerns. Later, his private world, or what he makes of "reality," or his way of viewing all sorts of people, events, and situations, as well as himself, can be seen to revolve around the narrow framework of an old constellation of beliefs and feelings.

The rigidity of the neurotic's structure of thought is partly to be identified with the excessive consistency with which it operates as a filter for the subject's view of his experience. The structure of thought is also rigid in the respect that all the conflicting beliefs and emotions that make it up become active when one does: the Rat Man cannot consider himself to be frustrated without fixing on some person as interfering, and being angry at him or her and wanting to get rid of him; he cannot be angry at a supposed rival without considering himself guilty and deserving of punishment.

What is remarkable about the "indestructibility" of a neurotic structure of thinking is closely related to its rigidity and ubiquitousness. It is not surprising that some of a person's current beliefs should be, vaguely, traceable to his early training and experience, or that they should be found, in Freud's phrase, to "go back to"[2] beliefs he had early in life. It is not greatly surprising that a man should continue to hold some beliefs and emotions regarding, for example, his father and his relation to his father "on a few subjects," or that he should sometimes express or act on them. The neurotic's capacity, indirectly and "unconsciously," to express and act on his primary beliefs and emotions as if they were still in accordance with his situation, although they are not, may seem strange, but is not in itself unique. Freud, for example, could himself make out a dream-report to mean that his and his father's roles were reversed, and in "associating" glory over his father and make fun of him, although his father was not only no longer in a position of authority over him, but had recently died.[3]

But if, as Freud thought, his adult "megalomania" and "rebelliousness" against the "higher authorities"—and against people in positions that they might not be deserving—"went back to" his childhood pride and unexpressed defiance toward his father, and although in the interpretation of a dream the second could be found to "lie behind" the first, and the second could be said to be still present, it is clear that his adult attitude was, so to speak, on its own. Freud could exercise his "megalomanic" disposition without referring to his father; he could express or act on it without feeling as if he were expressing something in regard to his father or as if he were acting in regard to him. He disliked it in itself, and it had its own validity; it could not be reduced to the childhood attitude.

Freud was at first amazed to find that the Rat Man's father was dead. Perhaps this was in part because he was discovering that the Rat Man's fundamental beliefs and emotions centering on his relation to his father were still in force, and that he was preoccupied with them to the exclusion of an independent view of his experience. The patient's first-level, apparently contemporary attitudes were closely tied to his primary beliefs and emotions. The Rat Man could not, for example, be angry at a person whom he saw as standing in the way of his courtship without feeling as if he were guilty of murderous designs on his father. His habit of taking people to be standing in the way of his erotic success had no validity of its own, and was practically reducible to his beliefs that his father was interfering, that he could not have any erotic satisfaction without disobeying his father, and so on.[4]

And, probably, Freud's amazement is partly accountable in terms of the constancy with which the Rat Man was viewing through the filter of, expressing, and acting upon the primary constellation of beliefs and feelings. For such beliefs sometimes to be active is not strange, but for the subject to be obsessed by them, for him continually to be seeing them as illustrated or realized, and for him constantly to be expressing and acting on them as if they were in accordance with his present situation, when in fact they are almost totally irrelevant to it—that is strange, and requires explanation.

132

1. "UNCONSCIOUS"

Freud held in theory that "ideas" are either conscious or unconscious at any given moment, and that there is no intermediate "state" between consciousness and unconsciousness. He held that although all of a person's ideas that are not at the moment conscious are then unconscious, the term "unconscious" may be reserved for ideas that are incapable easily, at any time, or under normal circumstances, of becoming conscious, while those that are momentarily unconscious but can at any time, easily, or under normal circumstances, become conscious may be designated "preconscious." By this view, ideas are divided into systems according to whether or not they are normally capable of becoming conscious, and the Ucs. is set aside, out of contact with the remainder of the psyche, and "buried" and prevented from becoming conscious by "barriers," "forces of defense," a "censorship," or "anticathexes."[5]

Considering some common examples of its application to cases, a surface similarity appears between a non-Freudian view of being unconscious and Freud's theoretical view. A person who is said to be "unconscious of the impending storm" or "of the tense atmosphere in the room" or "of his wife's signal" or "of his own vanity" usually, at least, seems to be one who just does not see—notice, perceive, or comprehend—the storm, atmosphere, signal, or vanity. It would seem that a part of a non-Freudian usage of "unconscious" is that it covers unqualified unawareness, not knowing, being ignorant of or oblivious to something; it may be that for this usage the paradigm case is being out cold. The adverb seems commonly to mean inadvertently, unwittingly, and/or without at all noticing or recognizing. In this respect the view of "being unconscious" that the non-Freudian usage implies seems similar to Freud's "buried" theoretical view.

But the non-Freudian usage carries no implications as to whether the "idea" in question is capable of becoming conscious. This is, I think, because what is ordinarily covered by the terms "conscious" and "unconscious" is not the state of an idea, but a person's state of awareness or unawareness—of an event, action, circumstance, belief, assumption, assessment, inclination, attitude, or whatnot.

To make the subject's state of awareness central rather than the state (condition, psychical location) of an idea changes the picture of what "being conscious" or "unconscious" is in no trivial way. One point it affects is the question of what possible "states" there are. It might be possible to argue that (at a given moment) an idea must be either conscious or unconscious, and that there are no intermediate possibilities. But clearly a person may be more or less fully aware of the state of the weather, his wife's gestures, his own vanity, and so on.

Freud's usage of "unconscious" in reporting and interpreting particular cases is quite different from the non-Freudian use and from what his theory would imply. But what he covers by it, which figures in his interpretations of dreamers and neurotics, resembles the non-Freudian usage in the respect that it is called so in accordance with the subject's state of awareness or unawareness. He called Elisabeth von R.'s love of her brother-in-law unconscious because Elisabeth could express and act upon it, and tell over her memories in such a way that it became evident to Freud, without herself (fully) recognizing that she loved the man. He called the Rat Man's hostility to his father "unconscious" because the subject did not formulate it or express it "straight out," and denied it, although indirectly he expressed and acted on it and imposed it (with the structure of beliefs and emotions of which it was a part) upon his experience in "reality." What Freud in practice covered by the term "unconscious" can be partially characterized as being some belief, emotion, desire, group or structure of beliefs and emotions, or the like that the subject can express, act on, or view a dream-report, situation, event or person in terms of without becoming fully aware of it and without fully recognizing that he is doing so. The belief or emotion is "unconscious" in that the subject is not fully aware of it; he does not clearly recognize, formulate, acknowledge, or explicitly state it.[6]

Like cases considered from the point of view of a non-Freudian usage of "conscious" and "unconscious," Freud's cases illustrate not just two possible states of awareness, but a continuum; they show, in fact, that there are many ways and degrees of being aware and unaware. The idiosyncracy of Freud's usage of "unconscious" as applied to specific cases begins to appear when it is seen that what he calls "unconscious" is a continuum.

He uses "unconscious" to cover various ways and degrees of being unaware, from something like the patient's love of the professor[7] (which she sometimes fully recognized and acknowledged, and openly, though against her judgment, acted on, but which she could view a dream-report in terms of without recognizing it, though she agreed when the significance of her "associations" was pointed out to her); to something like his own "megalomania"[8] and his dislike of it, which he was never fully aware of expressing or acting upon, or viewing through the filter of, except in "interpreting dreams" and the like—that is, by drawing conclusions from his own "associations" as applied to dream-reports, and from his spontaneous commentary on what the "associations" were revealing—but which he did find, then, without anyone's pointing them out to him; to something like the Rat Man's fundamental, conflicting beliefs and emotions (which he never, until the end, fully recognized in his behavior, reflections, or memories, and which he did not acknowledge or credit when they had repeatedly been pointed out to him as an "inevitable interpretation," the more inevitable as it was found to be the constant underlying interpretation of his neurotic behavior and thinking).

Freud would probably object that while what he termed "unconscious" in reporting and interpreting specific cases or fragments of cases may constitute a graded series—so that it could be said that some of the beliefs and emotions he called "unconscious" were "more unconscious" than others—the impression is owing to the "harmless looseness of phraseology"[9] that he often employed: some of the instances (the patient's love?) should, strictly, have been said to involve "preconscious ideas."

But the cases overrule such an objection. The point that Freud's instances of "the unconscious" comprise a continuum, like what is ordinarily opposed to "unconscious" but unlike what is ordinarily called unconscious, is important because it points to a central difference between what Freud called "unconscious" and what is unconscious in a non-Freudian sense. What is unconscious in another sense does not comprise a graded series because it is just unknown. What Freud calls "unconscious" is not unknown.

In cases in which a non-Freudian might call a person "unconscious," it may make sense to ask whether the subject is capable of becoming aware of that which he does not know or perceive or comprehend, and the question might often be answered in the negative: many cases of being unconscious are cases in which the subject could not be aware, because of circumstances (what he is unconscious of is in the future, or outside his line of view, or could only be perceived or understood by one who has information which he lacks) or because of an inability or defect on his part, which may fall under some such heading as physical incapacity (deafness, near-sightedness), stupidity, dullness, lack of sympathy or concern for others, and so on.

But in Freud's cases, what is "unconscious" is never something that the subject could not be aware of, know, or comprehend. In the first place, what Freud refers to as "unconscious" is some desire, belief, or the like of the subject's; second and more important, it is tacitly recognized by him. The Rat Man behaved strangely when he denied Freud's hypothesis that he had been very angry with his father as an interferer; he then told a story about a woman who killed herself when she caught herself wishing for the death of a close relative so as to gain a husband, and said that he felt like her, and that he too deserved to die for his thoughts. He continued to deny that he had ever been in the least hostile toward his father. But it was not the case that he was so lacking in logic that he could not comprehend his own emotions when his expression of them was pointed out to him. He was a highly intelligent, "clearheaded" person:[10] his lack of reason in this instance consisted in refusing to accept or, in one sense, recognize the emotions that at the same time he implicitly recognized and all but explicitly acknowledged.

If any of the beliefs, emotions, and desires in terms of which Freud interprets particular cases qualifies as "unconscious," the Rat Man's structure of beliefs and emotions regarding his father does, but he was not unaware of it. His awareness of it was not only shown by his tacit acknowledgement of his hostility toward his father, and his nearly explicit assessment of it as so wrong that he deserved to die for it (not only in one instance), but also by the guilt he suffered, which could only be understood as guilt over it, and by his repeated nearly suicidal, self-punishing behavior (which at the same time indirectly expressed his hostility), and by his very attempts, in the course of psychoanalysis, not to have to face his hostile attitude or his belief that it was monstrous and dangerous. One cannot be preventing himself from recognizing, formulating, or directly acting on or openly expressing a structure of emotions and beliefs, and feeling guilt over it and punishing oneself for entertaining it, without being at least partially or vaguely aware of it.

No general account can be given of the extent or degree of people's awareness and unawareness of "unconscious" emotions and beliefs. An account can be given only by referring to particular cases. And the cases are a graded series; the extent of awareness and unawareness varies, and the respects in which a given subject is aware and unaware differ from the respects in which another subject knows and does not know.

Where "unconscious" is used as Freud used it, to cover cases like his, it is impossible to draw any clear line between being "conscious" and "unconscious," or to say precisely what "becoming conscious" (as against being "unconscious") would constitute. What Freud calls being "unconscious" may be being aware of a belief or emotion in the respect that one will clearly recognize it, and make it explicit, when he attends to his own "associations" as applied to a primary text, but evades clear recognition of what he is doing when he otherwise expresses it or views in its terms; or it may be avoiding clear recognition or direct formulation until one is presented with an interpretation that attributes it to him, when he will acknowledge it. Freud's subjects may vaguely recognize a belief but not admit to it or express it "straight out"; "recognize" in this connection has at least two senses: one may recognize in the sense of noticing or perceiving or even admitting to, and not recognize in the sense of allowing, crediting, or accepting. ("It can't be true"; or, "It seems to be true, but I can't believe it.") Did Elisabeth von R. become conscious (as against "unconscious") of her love for her brother-in-law when Freud first told her his interpretation of her memories, talk, and behavior, or when she admitted that his interpretation seemed to be correct, or when she stopped trying to deny her love and began to recognize it in the sense of crediting and accepting it as her own emotion?

What Freud's cases of being "unconscious" have in common is just that, in each of them, the subject could have been expected to become fully aware when he does not, or he could have been expected to express more openly, acknowledge or take note of more readily, act on more explicitly, and formulate with less prodding than he requires. It invariably appears that he dislikes, or fears and loathes, the emotions, beliefs, and desires that he is "unconscious" of. Hence, to the extent that he does not know, his not knowing (and not making explicit, overt, direct) can be explained as wanting not to know.

Freud's theoretical account of "the unconscious" not only does not fit his cases. It takes out of consideration the central point that he is always noting when he refers to a belief or desire, an emotion-cluster or structure of thought as "unconscious": that the subject does not become fully aware of it, and does not formulate or express or act on it explicitly or directly,

138

because he would prefer not, or wants not, to know it. The point of calling the Rat Man's hostility, or his structure of beliefs and emotions, "unconscious" was to stress that he could implicitly act on, think in terms of, express, or even deplore it without becoming fully aware of it, because it was unthinkable to him. This point is totally obscured by the theory that unconscious ideas are inadmissible to consciousness and lead their own existence, cut off from the remainder of the psyche.

And Freud's theoretical division between "unconscious" and "preconscious" does not suit his cases. He does not deal with material that fits his definition of the "preconscious" any more than he deals with unconscious "ideas."

The patient's love of the professor would seem to qualify for the category of "preconscious," because she was sometimes fully aware of it (she openly discussed it and acted upon it with full understanding that she was doing so) and sometimes not. But it was neither the case that, when "unconscious" of it, she was quite unaware of it, nor the case that she could easily, at any time, become fully aware of it. The point of calling her love for the man "unconscious" was that she could make out a dream-report to mean that he came to visit her without being fully aware that she was doing so, and could provide "associations" leading to the establishment of that meaning without fully recognizing their tendency (until it was pointed out), because she preferred not to be aware of her emotion. This point would be erased by calling her love "preconscious," which would be to say that it might be temporarily unknown or out of mind (the implication of the theoretical model is: while the subject was otherwise occupied), but could in any ordinary circumstances become "conscious" as against "unconscious." It seems likely that her sometimes "unconsciousness" could be accounted for by its occurring in circumstances in which it was easy to avoid full recognition, by failing to draw a conclusion or take note of an inexplicit tendency; she did not dislike it so much as to put up a greater struggle.

Freud was not dealing with *ideas* that could be relegated to one "system" or another, and he was not dealing with emotions, beliefs, and desires that were unknown or that could become fully conscious at any time. Another example of something that is sometimes fully conscious and sometimes "unconscious" in a way the theory covers up is that of Elisabeth von R.'s opposition to her love for her brother-in-law—that is, her hatred of it or of herself for entertaining it, or her belief that it was monstrous and an offense to her family; or her moral scruples and devotion to her family; or her "whole moral being." All this was neither "preconscious" (capable at any time of becoming [fully] conscious) nor "unconscious" (incapable in ordinary circumstances of becoming conscious): it could be acted upon as opposition or "resistance" without the subject's becoming fully aware of it. She wanted not to know that her moral scruples and sense of duty to and love of her family were outraged by her love of her brother-in-law, or that she believed that an emotion of hers was monstrously offensive; in this connection, she wanted not to be, and was not, fully aware of her moral scruples, sense of duty, or "whole moral being," and she went very much further than the patient just mentioned in denying them. But she could easily enough become fully aware of her standards and scruples, her "moral being," and even her assessment of such a love (that would be very wrong) except insofar as to be aware of it entailed being aware that she did love the man and did believe that she was wicked.

It is not, in any of these cases, that the subject is ignorant or oblivious, but would dislike the belief or emotion in question if he did become aware of it and would be sorry to know of it. It is rather that the subject is, at least, putting off recognizing the belief or emotion or opposing or conflicting attitudes in question, and keeping himself from having to formulate or state them, even to himself, because he does, at least, dislike them and does not want to know about them. *He is actively avoiding having to become fully conscious of them.*

The phenomena of "resistance," from the first cases in which Freud discovered it, should have made this point clear. Elisabeth, who told her story at first in such a way as to omit anything that could point to her love for her brother-in-law and what it meant to her, who later upon insistence would admit that she had been holding something back—which generally proved particularly indicative of her conflict—who later still exclaimed that it could not be true that she loved her sister's husband, for she was not so wicked, and who had to lose some of her hatred of the emotion before she could accept and credit it as her own, made clear that the "unconscious" is not unknown, and that as Freud himself said, *"Not knowing is not wanting to know."*[11]

The other patients of the same period, whose cases Freud summed up in the example of a woman about to recognize as undeniable an old sexual "wish" who distracts her own and the therapist's attention from it and almost disrupts the treatment by becoming aware instead of a similar desire in regard to the therapist, should have indicated that a central fact of neurosis is that the subject is doing whatever he can not to be fully aware of certain beliefs or feelings. The dream-interpretations, in which what the subject was indirectly revealing was regularly unrecognized by him at a point when he might have been expected to recognize it (and was regularly unrecognized and inexplicitly acted on and expressed in other circumstances) and in which the subject's dislike of or repugnance for what was revealed regularly became clear, should have made it clear that "the unconscious," in Freud's sense, is never that of which one is oblivious, but is always what one is avoiding. The later cases, as represented by Freud's case histories, should have made clear that not *a,* but *the* central fact of neurosis is that the subject is actively attempting, and doing whatever he can, not to become fully aware of a set of fundamental, conflicting beliefs and emotions.

The theoretical view of "the unconscious" as unknown or virtually out of mind—though stashed away somewhere and capable ultimately, in the "extraordinary circumstances" of psychoanalysis, of being uncovered—is most harmful in preventing a clear formulation of the central characteristic of "the unconscious": that it is what the subject actively avoids formulating, directly facing or recognizing, or openly and explicitly expressing and acting on. The concomitant theoretical division of "ideas" into those that are capable at any time, easily, under ordinary circumstances, of becoming conscious and those that are not is most harmful as standing in the way of a distinction among the various ways and degrees of being aware and unaware that Freud deals with under the heading of "unconscious," which would be relevant to the cases.

Some of the emotions, beliefs, and opposing or conflicting attitudes that Freud in practice calls "unconscious" are "more unconscious" than others. What is "most unconscious" in Freud's cases—that which is most consistently not recognized, with the greatest apparent obtuseness, or denied when presented as an interpretation or conclusion, most vigorously and with the greatest trouble to the subject "resisted" or "fended off" (led away from, covered up with distractions, avoided in "associating" or, for instance, reciting memories as well as being most scrupulously kept from direct expression or action or formulation)—is that which the subject most wants not to know, which he cannot bear to face, or which is "unthinkable" to him. For example, the Rat Man's fundamental beliefs and emotions regarding his father were "more unconscious" than Freud's beliefs that he was more worthy than his father and deserving of the higher position, but that to set himself above his father was impertinent and absurd—in short, his "rebellion" and his distaste for it—in the sense that Freud could recognize his old attitudes in his own "associations" to a dream-report and then not try to deny or repudiate them, but carry out their implications in some detail (and even, from his tone, with some relish), and publish them; whereas the Rat Man not only did not similarly draw conclusions from his own "associations," and not only did not acknowledge Freud's less and less tentative conclusions about his state of mind, but went to lengths of denial or repudiation that are exemplified in the accounts of how, after having tacitly acknowledged the correctness of one of Freud's "constructions" and having said that he deserved to die for his thoughts, he nevertheless denied that

142

he had ever had the slightest hostility toward his father; and how, after having recalled the story of his childhood beating and the epic of fantasy he had built around it, he refused to acknowledge that the event had taken place or that the beliefs and emotions epitomized in his memory had ever been his. The root difference is clear. Freud did not think it was very good of himself to rebel against his father, set himself above him, make fun of him, and glory over him, but he did not think it was very bad either; he only considered his "infantile" "megalomania" impertinent and absurd. In short, he preferred not to think about it, but did not struggle to remain unaware of it, because he could easily bear to face it. But the Rat Man could not bear to face his hostility toward his father as impediment. He thought it monstrous and very dangerous; he did struggle very hard and at great cost to himself not to be aware of it.

What is "most unconscious," then, in Freud's cases is not what is closest to being unknown, or what the subject is most nearly genuinely oblivious to or ignorant of. It is what he is trying most actively and constantly to keep himself unaware of. Contrary to the theoretical picture, it is what most occupies him. [12]

2. THE MEANING OF A SYMPTOM

If a neurotic's fundamental, conflicting, "unconscious" structure of beliefs, emotions, and desires is not unknown and not put aside and ignored, but greatly occupies the subject and is in constant operation, being imposed on and turning into situations of insoluble conflict the events that in theory revive and augment the "unconscious" and instigate the conflict, then the conflicting structure of thought is not preserved by its burial. How is it preserved then; why is it the "indestructible," rigid, constant filter through which the subject views his experience?

If the fundamental structure is not divided into that which will out and that which would block it, if no part of it, or the whole, can be imagined to be seeking to "force a way through," and if nobody could "regress" to it for satisfaction or consolation, nor does, but rather attempts to flee it, and if neurotic symptoms are not brought about by a process of "displacement" or translation to the end of pleasure or "discharge," and are not satisfactions, then neurotic symptoms are not to be explained as the overcoming of the censorship barrier by the swollen "unconscious" and its achievement of emergence, expression, and satisfaction. How are they to be explained?

In ordinary cases, a person who has a general belief or expectation, preconception, assumption, or prejudice will be more likely to experience a situation or event, person, and so on as an illustration or substantiation of it than one whose mind it never crossed. Seeing it illustrated or substantiated will bring it up, so to speak, and bring it more nearly home to the subject. Supposing that one had, for example, a vague suspicion that human begins are inherently evil: with that suspicion one will be comparatively likely to experience evilness in humans and in consequence the vague suspicion is likely to become a degree less vague, a degree less like suspicion, and more like (unshakable) belief. The subject—especially after experiencing several instances—will become more clearly aware of his belief and more likely to formulate it, or to formulate it more decisively than before (for example, as a truth instead of a suspicion: Thomas Hardy's epitaph, "Life's a jest and all things show it; I thought so once and now I know it"). And, while seeing people or events as illustrating or substantiating a belief has in general the effect of strengthening and making less tentative the belief, and bringing it to mind, making the subject more aware of it, it leads the subject at the same time to feel and act accordingly in the particular instance, and it leads him to be more on the look-out for further substantiations.

Many beliefs progress in this manner: already entertaining a belief, perhaps vaguely and tentatively, and without being fully aware of it, the subject experiences events and situations as illustrating it; it is thus in his view closer to confirmation, and at the same time, in general, to being fully conscious—that is, clearly recognized, formulated in the subject's mind and clearly stated to others, and acted on with the subject's full awareness that that is what he is doing. Holding it more firmly and recognizing it more clearly, he is more likely than before to see it substantiated in "reality"; the more he sees it as substantiated, the more it is brought home to him and the firmer and clearer it becomes, and so it grows.

The closest that Freud's cases come to supporting his theoretical view that the events he called "exciting causes" have the effect of throwing the subject back on his infantile unconscious wishes," or "material from the past," or augmenting "the unconscious," is that they show the neurotic to be imposing his "unconscious" set of beliefs and emotions on the events, or, in other words, experiencing the events as demonstrating, re-presenting, or realizing his beliefs and emotions. The events could be said in this respect to "activate" the conflicting emotions, beliefs, and desires: that is, to bring them home to the subject, make him less ignorant of them, and strengthen and confirm them. Hans, for instance, as I argued, must already have believed, at least vaguely and without greatly dwelling on the possibility, that his father might come to harm as a result of his own jealousy; other than such a belief, he had no reason to take the horse's collapse as meaning his father's downfall. And he must already have desired such a possibility and wanted it not to happen. Thus the event cannot be supposed to have taught him something new (or in at all the sense of the theory to have given force to his most fearful wishes, or his conflict). But such a dramatic presentation of the possible result of his conflicting emotions could hardly help but reinforce them and bring the possibility—and the beliefs and emotions—closer to home, or to consciousness.

I made the point, as against Freud's view of such events as being "exciting causes" of neurosis, neurotic illness, or accesses or outbreaks of flocks of symptoms, that the subject performs the same kind of seeing-as (and a similar responding-to) over and over—and, it would seem, he does so progressively. Hans' neurosis was ameliorated soon after his phobia appeared: that was his only out-and-out symptom. He did not have to go on seeing his "unconscious" conflict of beliefs and emotions realized or demonstrated in more and more experiences in "reality." But the Rat Man (and Freud's other adult neurotics) did, to the point where practically anything he mentioned could be interpreted as leading back to the fundamental pattern, and the pattern could be turned back further to interpret a vast variety of instances. He became, to use a phrase of Freud's, "marooned in the past," and there is reason to think that he got to that position by experiencing the present as realizing, demonstrating, or illustrating the old situation, or the old beliefs, or the old impossible choice between an infeasible and unreasonably imposed, and an unthinkable alternative. The more such a structure of thought is seen to be realized or demonstrated, the firmer it becomes and the less the subject can be ignorant of it, and the more he expects, and finds, its further confirmation; and so it grows.

In ordinary cases, certain beliefs sometimes become a person's primary means of sorting and labeling what he experiences. They may approach the status of a neurotic's fundamental beliefs in the respect that they become a constantly operative filter through which the subject views life. Such beliefs are often social, or political, or religious. They may or may not be open to revision in the face of glaring contradictions—and seldom are in the face of much-repeated lack of substantial confirmation; they may or may not, in effect, obsess the subject, that is, occupy him to the exclusion of most other considerations, being constantly dwelt on. They may be of very narrow scope and/or be ill related to one another, or they may form a broadly systematic world-view. They vary in many other respects. Probably not always, but often, they are what one wants to be correct, or thinks must be true. It need not be just that it would be pleasant, satisfying, or comfortable if such beliefs were true. It may be that the very meaning or significance of one's life in general seems to the subject to depend on certain beliefs being correct.

In cases of neurosis, the fundamental beliefs and emotions and desires are not pleasing or comfortable; they are not what the subject wants to see confirmed. The neurotic wants very much not to know about his "unconscious" beliefs and emotions; certainly he does not want to view his experience as representing or illustrating them. The neurotic wants not to know of his fundamental, conflicting beliefs and emotions. His not wanting to know is demonstrated in active "resistance": he does whatever he can in the course of psychotherapy, and also outside the therapeutic sessions, to keep himself from recognizing, formulating, explicitly expressing or acting on, or in any other way having to face head-on those beliefs and emotions. He is trying hard not to think of them. In general, trying hard not to think of something is a good way of preventing oneself from forgetting or ignoring it. The most plausible view of the persistence and the progressive imposition on experience of the neurotic's structure of thought would seem to be that he is caught in a vicious circle. Not only possessing the beliefs in question to begin with, but trying not to be aware of them, he experiences people, events, and situations as demonstrating, illustrating, epitomizing, or realizing them. Seeing events as illustrating his unwanted beliefs can hardly help but bring them home to the subject, and clarify and enforce them. In the ordinary case, the progression by means of seeing-as-substantiated is from tentativeness to reinforcement and, naturally, at the same time, from unawareness—lack of recognition, lack of formulation and clear expression—to clearer awareness. In the neurotic's case, the progressive substantiation of his primary beliefs must bring them progressively closer to being directly recognized or made explicit; it must make them more *in danger* of becoming fully conscious. Trying, then, even harder to prevent himself from being fully aware of his beliefs and emotions, the subject sees more and more—finally, in the most various, intrinsically harmless situations—the pattern as realized.

In short, it is more in accordance with Freud's cases of neurosis, as he reports and interprets them, to hold that the neurotic's "unconscious" beliefs, emotions, and desires are preserved and come exclusively to occupy the subject by his partly knowing and wanting not to know them, and by their operation in being imposed on his experience, than to hold that they are preserved by their burial. And it is more in accordance with his cases to hold that they "emerge"—that is, are seen by the subject as demonstrated or epitomized in actual situations, and are expressed and acted on—because no part or aspect of the person wants them to become conscious or explicit than to hold that they emerge, according to a principle of discharge or pleasure, by "forcing a way through."

From this perspective, neurotic symptoms can be regarded as responses to the subject's view of some event or situation as realizing or illustrating his fundamental "unconscious" beliefs—a response partly of acting on those beliefs and the emotions and desires they carry with them, but more prominently of trying not to be aware.

Freud's interpretations of particular cases of neurosis show that the subject views "reality"—a great part of what he encounters and experiences, and not just the events or situations that are designated "exciting causes"—through the filter of a set of "unconscious" beliefs, desires, and emotions. If the Rat Man's fundamental structure of thought was activated by his mother's plan, it was also activated, for example, by his conversation with the cruel army captain and the captain's mistaken direction to him (which he read mainly as representing the old dilemma between impossible obedience to his—cruel—father and unthinkable disobedience) and by Dick's visit to the lady and theft of her attention, the grandmother's taking her away from him by becoming ill, and her own coolness to him, in each of which instances the Rat Man saw himself as faced with the interferer who would deny him any erotic satisfaction, and was accordingly enraged at the obstacle-figure, and guilty over his rage.

Such illustrations or demonstrations of a pattern of thinking must have the effect of reinforcing it, solidifying it, and bringing it home to the subject, and making it more in danger of becoming explicit, clearly recognizable, and undeniable. If the

148

neurotic were not the way he is, he would on such occasions recognize and formulate or express the beliefs that seem to be confirmed. But to recognize these beliefs and emotions is just what he most wants not to do. He is "unconscious" of a structure of thought in the respect that he cannot bear to face it.

What he does in the face of an activating situation or event is not to recognize clearly the beliefs and emotions that it makes present; he could not bear to do so. And what he does is not to operate in terms of them in the same way that a man who finds another deceitful woman might act upon his conception of her and her kind, and the attendant emotional assessment. What he does is, for example, become unable to study, or embark on a frantic weight-losing program, or fall into an argument with himself and a vacillation in action between finding a way to follow a mistaken direction or not following it.

It seems at least a plausible view that all such courses are primarily extratherapeutic forms of "resistance," or of attempting to deny or repudiate, "fend off" or escape, and above all remain incompletely aware of the beliefs and emotions that are in danger of becoming fully conscious.

The interpretation of Hans' and the Rat Man's major symptoms indicated that they were attempts to escape, or prevent or avoid, an actual or possible situation that, to the subject, signified the primary conflict, or the results (or "satisfaction") of the conflicting, "unconscious" emotions and desires. But it seems likely that in such symptoms as Hans' phobia or the Rat Man's inability to study, the subject, by concentrating on the actual or possible situation or event or on something related to it such as, for instance, the Rat Man's studying (once an experience "in reality" has activated his conflicting beliefs and emotions by being read as realizing them), is also insisting that it is *this,* and not what it means to him, that he is concerned with. Hans, for example, is in effect insisting, and trying to persuade himself, that it is *horses* he is afraid of—what might happen to them—and *not* what might happen to his father or himself because of his love and jealousy. The Rat Man is insisting that his conflict with himself is that he wants to and must work, but cannot do it, and *not* (in part) that he wants to and must obey his father, but cannot.

Freud attributed Elisabeth von R.'s pains and difficulty in walking to her unwillingness to become aware of her love for her brother-in-law; what he tells of the occurrence of her symptoms suggests that the subject was able not to become fully aware of her love for the man—at times when it was most "in force" and hardest to deny—by concentrating upon her pain and disability. For example, these symptoms appeared suddenly and violently when she heard her brother-in-law's voice in the next room (a more directly activating situation than those mentioned in the later case histories).

Again, in the instance of the banting, the Rat Man seems to be insisting no, no, I'm not jealous or angry, I don't want to get Dick out of the way—I just want to get rid of *dick*![13]

The neurotic symptoms, then, may be regarded as a smoke screen, set up to confuse the issue and to keep the subject from having to face what he most wants not to know.

But the response—trying to prevent awareness—is itself made in terms of the beliefs, emotions, and desires that the subject is trying to prevent his awareness of, and while the symptom does apparently work as a smoke screen, it must also work as a further reinforcement. The Rat Man's response to the army captain, which was, in part, to consider himself commanded or obliged at once to carry out and not to carry out the man's mistaken direction to him, was just as much an illustration of his primary beliefs as the captain's talk and action presented to him; insisting on one's concern with an actual or possible situation that one reads as epitomizing emotions and beliefs that one wants not to know must tend to keep them in mind as well as to obscure them.

One reason why the smoke screen should also be an illustration, or the distraction an indication, is apparent: the subject, with difficulty fending off full awareness of what he wants not to know, seizes on something close to home; he could not put off full awareness by concentrating on something altogether disconnected from what does concern him. Also, he is operating in terms of the beliefs and emotions that he does not want to know. If a neurotic symptom can be considered primarily a denial or repudiation, it must still be considered secondarily a misconceived or misdirected action or expression—sometimes an acting on the subject's most fearful and repugnant emotions and desires, commonly a paying himself back for what he does know of what he wants not to know. If the Rat Man's weight-losing program can be considered primarily as a smoke screen, a denial of his rage at Dick (and at his father, the original interferer, seen in Dick's mild interference) by concentrating on the attempt to get rid of his fat, it can still be interpreted as an expression of the rage at Dick/the father, and more than that, as a self-punishment for that rage. But again, just as, and partly because, wanting not to see his beliefs substantiated, he sees situations as realizing them, and just as, in the same operation, wanting not to recognize his beliefs and emotions, he seizes as a smoke screen on what again illustrates them, in the same way, wanting to avoid what he might do, he does something analogous.

Freud's early formulation regarding the reason for and character of a neurotic symptom—"She spared herself the painful conviction . . . by inducing pains in herself"—was dropped. The self-distraction formula, never worked into the explicit theory, must have seemed a false lead, if indeed Freud gave it any further thought, when the theory of "wish-fulfillment" ("substitutive gratification," "compromise-formation") was developed. Another early formula, never worked into the central theory or seen as related to that of self-distraction, and dropped after the development of "wish-fulfillment," was that of "hysterical counter-will"; an example of this was Frau Emmy von N.'s tongue-clicking, which began when she was nursing a sick child, and "fear that she might make a noise turned into actually making one." Wanting to avoid what she might do, she did it.[14]

Just in itself, the distraction formula did leave unanswered questions that could be answered through a loose application of the "substitutive gratification" formula. When Freud said that

Elisabeth spared herself the painful conviction that she loved her sister's husband by giving herself pains, the question was left, why pains? Similarly, if Freud had said, simply, that the Rat Man tried to spare himself, or distract himself from, the recognition that he was in a jealous rage at Richard/wanting to get his interfering father out of the way by rushing about the country trying to get rid of his fat, he would have left the question, why in this way? Why by trying to get rid of something? Why fat? Why his fat?

Although, loosely applied, the "gratification" or "compromise" formula showed a way to answer such questions, it was itself a false lead. Like all Freud's stretchable terms, "wish-fulfillment," "substitutive gratification," and "compromise" survived because they could be used to cover something different from what, theoretically, they seemed to cover. That is, the "substitutive gratification" formula could be used instead of saying that the Rat Man's banting was an expression of hostility against Richard/his father, and at the same time a way of punishing himself for what he could not help recognizing of that hostility.[15] The theoretical context in which these terms evidently had a place—in which wishes and fulfillment, the metaphorical equivalents of excitation and discharge, were central, and in which neurotic conflict was reduced to the setting up of systematic barriers against the forcing through of wishes given power by regression—was thus perpetuated.

Part of my present point is that even the view of neurotic symptoms that was covered by the "fulfillment" and "substitution" formulas, not to speak of the formulas themselves, is shown by Freud's full interpretations of particular cases to be misleading in what it omits. The cases show that what primarily distinguishes the neurotic from others is not the strength of the "unconscious" beliefs, emotions, and desires that he wants not to know, express, or act on, but the extent or intensity of his wanting not to know. It is not that the beliefs and emotions that he hates and fears will out, or—simply—that his symptoms and neurotic behavior are indirect expressions and misdirected actions in terms of his "unconscious" structure of thought; it is rather that he is so afraid to face the primary beliefs and emotions that he does whatever he can to deny them, and in so doing ends up acting them out once more, while knocking himself on the head for his half an insight into them.

3. FREUD'S THEORY

When the theory of wishes and fulfillment is stripped away, what I have called the conflict theory remains. It can be summed up in a set of postulates or general formulations of the material discovered in Freud's cases of neurosis.

A. The neurotic views experience and responds to it in terms of a set (S) of interrelated beliefs, emotions, and desires.

B. S seem to go back to childhood.

C. S are in conflict; the subject cannot resolve the conflict by choosing one alternative and letting the other go, or accepting a compromise or other solution. For instance, he cannot choose to satisfy his sexual desires, because he believes that his father is opposed to his sexual activity and will punish it, and he loves and wants to obey his father: he cannot obey his father because he cannot give up all sexual desire, and the prohibition makes him angry; he is afraid of the results that his anger may bring about; he cannot avoid anger and disobedience to his father.

D. The subject considers himself monstrous and in danger for holding S.

E. He wants to be unaware of S, and actively attempts to deny, repudiate, avoid, and distract himself from them.

153

F. What he wants to be unaware of is by its content (e.g., one's father, love, sex) unavoidable. But concentrating on avoidance makes S more unavoidable, and leads the subject to see situations, events, and people as realizing the repudiated beliefs and emotions. And doing so reinforces them and makes him more aware of them. Trying the harder to avoid them, he reencounters them in more (and more diverse) situations, so that they come to occupy him constantly.

G. In making some move to avoid or deny what he wants not to know, the subject responds in terms of the same beliefs and emotions that he is avoiding: e.g., he sets himself contradictory commands, one of which is impossible to carry out, in an effort to escape or repudiate a situation that, to him, realizes repudiated beliefs and emotions; but the commands he sets himself illustrate S as well as the situation does.

H. Neurotic symptoms occur in situations in which the subject is most in danger of having to face S. They can be regarded as extra-therapeutic demonstrations of resistance, or smoke screens—the subject's attempts to deny, distract himself from, and avoid the beliefs and emotions of which he is in danger of becoming fully aware. And they can be regarded as actions based on those beliefs and emotions and his half-insight regarding them—usually a punishment for having them.

I. The neurotic's conflict is irresolvable primarily because he is in a vicious spiral of seeing and fleeing; psychoanalytic therapy can be considered to be directed primarily toward the subject's unlearning the habit of imposition or activation and flight. Toward this end the subject is brought to isolate the beliefs and emotions that he is imposing on reality and to see them for what they are. The process is gradual and interdependent with the subject's unlearning the habit of imposition and flight, and his isolation of his imposing beliefs and emotions is his learning to be less fearful of and opposed to them.

If this is Freud's theory, in what sense can it be used to explain? The conflict theory explains neurosis by revealing the *meaning of neurosis and of neurotic symptoms;* the explanation is an elucidation of neurosis and symptoms in terms of a structure of thought, its imposition on "reality," and a neurotic's attempts to repudiate and distract himself from it.

The postulates as such, however, explain neurosis only in the sense that they provide an outline of what is involved in neurotic illness and of what—generally speaking—symptoms, and neurotic behavior, obsessions, attacks, and so on, are symptomatic. They have the broadly coordinating function that Freud ascribed to his explicitly theoretical hypotheses; but, as applied to a particular case, the postulates can be used to explain or predict only quite vacuously. Given a case of neurosis, one could on the basis of the postulates predict the outline of its explanation: conflict, wanting not to know, a spiral of imposition and repudiation. Given a neurotic symptom, neurotic behavior, neurotic inability to act, or the like, one could predict the skeleton of its explanation by means of the postulates: imposition of and attempt to repudiate a pattern of beliefs and emotions, which ends in reinforcing them. But the postulates do not in themselves provide anything but such skeleton or outline explanations (and predictions); all one can tell about a particular case by applying the postulates to it is what that case has, or will prove to have, in common with others. And where the field of inquiry is neurosis and what its meaning may be, as compared, for instance, to billiard balls and why one ball goes a certain distance when struck by another, what a number of cases have in common does not shed much light on any one case. Hans' phobia, the Wolf Man's phobia (and his phase of religious obsessions and his neurotic collapse as a young man), Dora's symptoms, and the Rat Man's symptoms can all be explained by the postulates. But they are explained by the postulates in the same general way that actions can be explained in terms of the agent's intentions, purposes, motives, beliefs, and so on. To say that a man's actions can be explained by his intentions, etc., is not to say much about a particular man, or specific actions of his, unless the formula is filled in: what intentions? In much the same way, little Hans' phobia is not understood until it is known what particular beliefs and emotions are in conflict, filtering his view of his experience, and being repudiated; the Wolf Man's phobia is not understood until it is known *what* beliefs and emotions *he* is repudiating.

Given a hysterical attack or neurotic symptom, the psychoanalyst cannot predict what beliefs and emotions will be found to elucidate it; given a specific set of beliefs and emotions, he might predict what the interpretation of the subject's further symptoms and behavior will be, but not which symptoms or what behavior will be reported or exhibited; given the filled-out interpretation of one symptom (say, hysterical vomiting), he cannot predict the content (ingredients, filling out) of the interpretation of a very similar symptom in another patient. Psychoanalytic explanations are idiosyncratic.

What does illuminate a specific case of neurosis, or a neurotic symptom, is what fills in the outline provided by the postulates: the specific beliefs and emotions in conflict, in terms of which the subject is viewing his experience and responding to it. It was the material, in the cases of Dora, Hans, the Rat Man, the Wolf Man, that was providing an explanation.

The postulates are general formulations of the discoveries about particular subjects. They are mainly of use in providing a framework and guiding a form of inquiry by means of which the specific information can be elicited. They not only direct the psychoanalyst as to the sort of thing to expect and to look for in a case of neurosis, but, with an additional pair of working postulates that can be regarded as being derived from the theory, direct his manner of looking and his form of investigation. The additional postulates may be formulated as follows.

> J. Because the neurotic is repudiating or trying to deny, distract himself from, avoid, or escape S and hide them, he does not make them explicit in any way; they cannot be discerned in the evident tendency or aim of his behavior, and he does not state them. His direct declarations or avowals do not reveal them.

156

K. Because the neurotic becomes occupied with S to the exclusion of other concerns and is constantly imposing them on his experience (seeing diverse situations as revealing them) and responding, indirectly, in their terms, even in trying to escape them—because of this, if one listens long enough to his indirect statements, or to what is implicit in his answers to questions like "What does that make you think of?" or "How do you feel about that?" S will begin to become clear as an underlying pattern.

The filling in of the outline—the information gained through Freud's investigative approach as to the content of a particular structure of conflicting beliefs and emotions—explains a case of neurosis (Hans', the Rat Man's) and its symptoms, in the respect that it makes clear the meaning of the symptoms. It answers questions like these: What did Hans see in the horses, or the Rat Man in Dick? In terms of what beliefs and emotions was Hans regarding horses, or the Rat Man Richard? What is the meaning of the subject's response: Hans' inability to go outdoors, the Rat Man's reducing program? What was Hans, or the Rat Man, trying to do and not to do?

When the analyst has answers to questions like these, he has a pattern of thought. And when he has a pattern of thought, he can understand as related to one another a great number of instances of thinking, feeling, acting, and not acting, most of which seem unrelated and, from an ordinary point of view, would be considered totally unrelated.

NOTES

CHAPTER 1

1. First published in *Neurologisches Centralblatt,* 12(1), 4–10 (sections I and II), and 12(2), 43–7 (sections III–V). (January 1 and 15).

2. First published Leipzig and Vienna: Deuticke. All quotations below are from *The Standard Edition of the Complete Works of Sigmund Freud,* 24 vols. (hereafter cited as *Standard Edition*). Translated from the German under the General Editorship of James Strachey, in collaboration with Anna Freud, assisted by Alix Strachey and Alan Tyson. London: Hogarth Press and the Institute of Psycho-Analysis, 1953–77. Vol. II: *Studies on Hysteria* (hereafter cited as *Studies*).

3. *Studies,* p. 8.

4. *Ibid.,* p. 92.

5. *Ibid.,* p. 132.

6. *Ibid.,* p. 202 (Breuer's italics).

7. The concepts of affect and (nervous) excitation at times became indistinguishable. As nervous excitation was, so to speak, a shadow of affect, and as the authors thought, as Breuer said, that it was "self-evident that . . . acute affects go

along with an increase in cranial excitation" (*Studies*, p. 201), the terms "affect" and "excitation" could be and were used interchangeably. In a brief passage the authors could begin by discussing affect, shift into nervous excitation, and switch back to affect. The same story could be told in two locations, or somewhere between them.

8. "Abreaction" or "catharsis" was also used in a more general sense to cover any case of relief from emotion through expression.

9. For instance, what happens to the memory of a frightening accident when recalled after the event in association with the further memory of rescue and the consciousness of present safety. The authors, true to their fundamental concept, did not consider that a person ceased to feel fearful because he came to understand that the danger was past and unlikely to recur, but believed that the affect was dissipated through "thought activity."

10. A "hypnoid state" was supposed to be a condition of somnambulance, in which—precisely—reaction was impossible and there was no "association" with the contents of normal consciousness.

11. The authors did not make it entirely clear *how* they thought an idea carrying an amount of undischarged affect could become the cause of a hysterical symptom. They suggested, however, at least two possibilities. (1) The quantity of affect, prevented from finding normal release, leaked out in the form of a symptom; the symptom was an abnormal expression of emotion. (2) The quantity of nervous excitation corresponding to the dammed-up affect brought about the "motor innervation," which was visible as a symptom.

12. *Studies*, p. 99.

13. *Ibid.*, p. 174.

14. *Ibid.*, p. 202.

CHAPTER 2

1. First published in *Neurologisches Centralblatt,* 13(10), 362–4, and (11), 402–7 (May 15 and June 1). Quotations below from

Standard Edition, Vol. III: *Early Psycho-Analytic Publications.*

2. *Studies*, p. 286.

3. "The Neuro-Psychoses of Defense," pp. 60–61.

4. Freud retained essentially the same theory of repression until the end of his career; see, for instance, the metapsychological paper on "Repression."

5. *Studies*, p. 280.

6. *Ibid.*, p. 285.

7. Freud discusses the influence of Bernheim on him in *Studies*, pp. 108–11 and 286–92.

8. *Ibid.*, p. 268.

9. *Ibid.*, p. 271. The device in itself was borrowed from Bernheim, but not Freud's idea of what it accomplished. It was not through Bernheim that Freud came to suppose that the patient's "will" had to be distracted in order for him to recall what he had ostensibly forgotten.

10. He could have introduced the term before this point in the case; the concept had already been implied.

11. *Studies*, p. 156.

12. *Ibid.*

13. *Ibid.*, p. 159.

14. *Ibid.*, p. 157.

15. *Ibid.*, p. 159.

16. *Ibid.*, p. 166.

17. *Ibid.*, p. 268. (Freud's italics.)

18. *Ibid.*, pp. 269–70.

19. *Ibid.*, p. 157.

20. *Ibid.*, p. 167.

21. *Ibid.*, p. 157.

22. The equation continued, in theoretical formulations, for a remarkably long time: it was perpetuated through a theoretical division of mental activities into systems or agencies. Although Freud seemed always to assume that desires attributable to the Ego could be unconscious in the same sense as the most objectionable "ideas" when he was interpreting individual cases, his theory was unable to accommodate the practical postulate until, in *The Ego and the Id* (1923), Freud recognized the "unconscious Ego."

23. *Studies,* p. 291.
24. *Ibid.,* p. 283.
25. *Ibid.,* p. 157.
26. *Ibid.,* p. 282.
27. *Ibid.,* p. 159.
28. *Ibid.,* p. 304.
29. Freud, however, explicitly repudiated this concept. He held that either an idea was conscious, or it was not. (The slightly later concept of the "preconscious" was an idea that might easily become conscious, as distinguished from the "unconscious," which might not.)
30. Freud later made this point, but stated it in the language of affective ideas (or a lineal descendant) and made it seem to depend on that concept. He said that when the therapist informs a patient that he has a certain "idea" that he has repressed, the patient does not thereby become conscious of the repressed idea. At first there may be, in two different localities of his mental apparatus, two ideas of identical content. He becomes conscious of the repressed idea only when it itself is perceived by him. ("The Unconscious," *Standard Edition,* Vol. XIV, p. 175.)
31. *Studies,* p. 157.
32. *Ibid.,* p. 164.
33. *Ibid.,* p. 174.
34. *Project for a Scientific Psychology, Standard Edition,* Vol. I (Pre-Psycho-Analytic Publications and Unpublished Drafts), pp. 295–6 (hereafter cited as *Project*).
35. "To furnish a psychology that shall be a natural science: that is, to represent psychical processes as quantitatively determinate states of specifiable material particles, thus making those processes perspicuous and free from contradiction," *Project,* p. 295.
36. "The Unconscious," Vol. XIV, p. 174. Freud did not give up the belief that some equation translation might some day be possible.
37. *Studies,* pp. 186–7.
38. "The Unconscious," pp. 180–1. Freud distinguishes "descriptive" from "systematic" meanings by employing abbrevi-

ations Cs., Ucs, Pcs. when referring to systems. For fuller discussion see Chapter 3.

39. The first chapter is a review of the literature on dreams; the sixth is transitional between the mediating and hard-quantity theories.

40. In the libido theory, Freud carried out the lead already provided in the processes theory by the "pleasure principle" and applied the hypothesis of quantity to the person as a whole. He postulated a total quantity of psychic sexual energy, as a whole capable of increase (through somatic changes or strangulation, that is, damming up) and decrease (through somatic changes or discharge), something like displacement (fixation), and regression. At the same time he was using the hypothesis of quantity in nearly its original sense, to account, among other things, for repression. He was supposing that desires, for instance, can be considered as ideas plus or minus cathexis, and that an idea's charge of excitation can undergo certain vicissitudes. The main new attempted fusion was between the two uses of the central hypothesis, and it did not work. Here it was not even so much the case that central concepts were hovering between their ingredients as that Freud vacillated between the newer and the older uses of the hypothesis of quantity, and never at all clearly defined the concepts of fixation, repression, and regression as they had to be defined, as fusing the two uses. Freud's concept of the sexual instinct or instincts was on the whole in accordance with the newer uses of the hypothesis, but when he asked himself how the sexual instinct, or one of its components, could be repressed, he had to suppose that not the instinct or impulse—a constantly renewed quantity of psychical sexual excitation—but an idea that, by being cathected with that excitation had become the "instinct-representative," could be repressed. At the same time Freud was supposing that an idea, in order to be repressed, had to be deprived of its libidinal cathexis, so that what made an idea an instinct-representative had to be removed when it, or, loosely speaking, the instinct was repressed. This can be attributed not only to the failure of fusion, but also to the old problem that the counters and possi-

162

ble moves were too few: excitation (its strangulation, removal, fixation, regression, displacement, and discharge) had too much work to do. The confusion as to psychical representatives—and indeed, the whole web of multiplied confusions— is also symptomatic of the explanation by multiplication of processes and "particles" that characterize the quantity direction, so that what seems on the one hand to be abstracting the essential factors from the material of observation to make it clear and free from contradiction also seems to explain it in terms of background processes going on in another arena or arenas (here the body and the limbo of the quantity-process psyche).

41. "The Unconscious," Vol. XIV, pp. 174–6. In other, rather similar passages on the same question, he does not so much shift as hover, with the result that neither the quantitative nor the practical considerations are so clear as in the passage above. Cf. *Introductory Lectures*, Vol. XVI, pp. 436–7.

CHAPTER 3

1. *Standard Edition*, Vol. V: *The Interpretation of Dreams*, p. 461. This book was first published by Franz Deutiche. Leipzig and Vienna, 1900. In the English *Standard Edition*, Vols. IV and V.

2. Some of the earliest versions of this point (when Freud still in theory considered the "pathogenic material" to consist in the memories of "traumatic events") were in the papers "Heredity and the Aetiology of the Neuroses" and "Further Remarks on the Neuro-Psychoses of Defense," both published in 1896. (*Standard Edition*, Vol. III.)

3. So Freud stated this discovery in a letter to Fliess of 1896. (*Standard Edition*, Vol. I, p. 239.)

4. This was the "Secret of Dreams," definitely decided upon in 1900. (*Interpretation of Dreams*, p. 121n.) The analogy between dreams and neurotic symptoms was developing at the

period of the *Project for a Scientific Psychology* and the Fleiss papers, between 1894 and 1899, as the Editors point out in the introduction to *Interpretation of Dreams*.

5. *Standard Edition*, Vol. I.

6. *Three Essays on the Theory of Sexuality*, 1905, came between the theory of primary and secondary processes and the libido theory; in later editions it was made to incorporate parts of the latter. (*Standard Edition*, Vol. VII.)

7. Compare the relationship between emotion (affect) and nervous excitation in the earliest hysteria theory.

8. *Interpretation of Dreams*, Vol. V, p. 598.

9. *Ibid.*, p. 605.

10. *Ibid.*, p. 595.

11. *Ibid.*

12. *Ibid.*, p. 596.

13. *Ibid.*

14. *Ibid.*

15. *Ibid.*, p. 597.

16. Because, when he talks, for instance, about the interpretation of symptoms, Freud has to become more specific as to the mental factors that are involved, he introduces into contexts dominated by the libido theory "desires," "wishes," and "ideas," as well as the intermediate "impulses." How can an "idea" be related to the sum of psychical sexual energy? Obviously, the energy must cathect the idea. Something like the original sense of the hypothesis of quantity is thus introduced alongside its modification; ideas are supposed to be the vehicles, or "psychical representatives," of the sexual instinct, or of libido (which is itself the psychical representative of somatic excitation). The two conceptions are not very securely fused; the lack of fusion is illustrated by considerable vagueness in the definition of certain central concepts. For example, how, beyond saying that a part of the total quantity of libido is left behind, can fixation be defined? Within the *Introductory Lectures*, Freud sometimes says that a portion of libido remains attached to a pregenital organization or primary object; sometimes that a part of the quantity remains attached to certain

164

unconscious ideas or libido-representatives, or to old paths to satisfaction, or to a point in its development, or to certain instinct-tendencies, as to childhood experiences or impressions. The lack of fusion is also illustrated by various problems or incoherences. For instance, Freud wanted to say that libido, the sexual instinct, or a component-instinct was repressed, as repression at the point of fixation was an essential ingredient of the theory, and it was libido or the instinct that could be said to be fixated, and regress; he did often say so. But, in his paper on "The Unconscious," he ran up against the difficulty that sexual energy, or an instinct in his sense, was incapable of being an "object of consciousness," and therefore could not be made unconscious, or repressed. He solved the problem with the idea. To say that an instinct was repressed, he concluded, was to employ a "harmless looseness of phraseology," for an idea could be the psychical representative of the instinct, and an idea could be repressed. One of the main troubles with his solution was that he was at the same time treating repression as the removal from an idea of its excitation—i.e., at this point, libido. ("The Unconscious," in *Standard Edition,* Vol. XIV: *On the History of the Psycho-Analytic Movement. Papers on Metapsychology and Other Works,* p. 177.)

17. Freud later distinguished, officially formulated in *The Ego and the Id* (1923), not so much between the systems Ucs. and Pcs. as between the "Id" and the "Ego." The Id was considered to be the part, aspect, and mentality of infantile, unconscious wishes, with offshoots in the preconscious; the Ego was described in about the same terms as what I am calling here the preconscious-adult. Although Freud came to consider the Ego to be partially "unconscious," there was no substantial change in his conception of the two aspects from what is outlined here, nor in his ways of formulating what it is for an "idea" or "wish" to be "unconscious." The major changes in the new structural model consisted of officially recognizing unconscious components of the Ego and in introducing the Super Ego.

18. The technique of "free association" was, of course, the

descendant of such devices as the "pressure technique" (or, in general, the eliciting of whatever might come to the patient's mind in connection with the time when his symptoms originated), and ultimately of the use of hypnosis to bring the "pathogenic ideas" to expression. Though Freud now saw the neurotic symptom or dream as related to the "unconscious material" as fulfillment to desire (or act to wish), and hence considered himself to be discovering by "free association" not what events had caused a symptom but what it meant and why it was produced, he conceived of the technique in the same way as the earlier ones in this respect: it was a way of getting to the pathogenic material, which was certainly present but certainly not to be reached by way of "conscious purposive ideas"—which was, so to speak, below the surface (the surface being occupied and controlled, in effect, by the Ego, and the "pathogenic" being that which the Ego would exclude).

19. Freud placed some emphasis in the first part of *The Interpretation of Dreams* on certain dreams, usually of children, that could be called recognizable representations of wishes as fulfilled.

20. *Interpretation of Dreams,* Vol. IV, p. 122.

21. *Ibid.,* p. 235.

22. *Ibid.,* Vol. V, p. 478.

23. *Ibid.,* p. 461.

24. *Ibid.,* Vol. IV, p. 219.

25. *Ibid.,* Vol. V, pp. 565–6; p. 598; other passages in Chapter VII.

26. *Ibid.,* Chapter VII, especially pp. 565–6; 598–9.

27. *Ibid.,* Chapter VII, e.g., pp. 594–8; 602–5; 607; 616–7. In *The Interpretation of Dreams,* Freud writes of the "unpleasure principle"; later he called it the "pleasure principle."

28. *Ibid.,* Chapter VII, e.g., pp. 566–7; 599–603.

29. *Ibid.,* Chapter VII, especially pp. 600–6.

30. *Ibid.,* Chapter VII, e.g., pp. 594–8; 603–5.

31. *The Interpretation of Dreams.*

32. *The Interpretation of Dreams.*

33. Its counterpart in the wish-fulfillment level of the new theory is sometimes identified as the Ego.

34. *The Interpretation of Dreams,* Chapter VII, especially pp. 567–82; 597–608.

35. For this and the following points, see the quotations in section 2 above.

36. See, for instance, *The Interpretation of Dreams,* pp. 540–2. See also the *Introductory Lectures* and the case histories throughout, and the clinical papers.

37. E.g., *The Interpretation of Dreams,* p. 548; pp. 576–7. This, and the further characterization of the two agencies summarized in the following two paragraphs, is clearly Freud's position in the *Introductory Lectures* and case histories; it is explicit, but it is not explicitly presented as official theory.

38. Freud seems to suppose that *wishing,* as distinct from wanting or—the more general term—desiring, could be regarded as characteristic of young children on the ground that their desires, while intense and pressing (brooking no delay in satisfaction) and in this respect wantlike, are like wishes in the respect that they may be "idle": children often desire without regard for feasibility, appropriateness, steps to be taken, and the like, without any notion of going about to obtain that which they desire and without regard for "reality."

39. E.g., *The Interpretation of Dreams,* Vol. IV, pp. 247, 250, 267.

40. E.g., *The Interpretation of Dreams,* p. 250; *On Dreams, Standard Edition,* Vol. V, e.g., p. 679.

41. *The Interpretation of Dreams,* Vol. V, p. 534. Compare *On Dreams,* p. 678.

42. *The Interpretation of Dreams,* Vol. IV, p. 308. On the other hand, the process of dream-formation ("dream-work") is described as essentially "primary," in anticipation of the view that it shows the characteristics of an infantile mode of expression. Who did it?

43. *Ibid.,* Vol. V, Chapter VI.

44. *Ibid.,* Vol. IV, p. 247.

CHAPTER 4

1. *Notes Upon a Case of Obsessional Neurosis* in *Standard Edition,* Vol. X: *Two Case Histories* (1909), p. 188; further discussion on p. 189.

2. *Ibid.,* pp. 165–73; 210–20. In particular, p. 169.

3. *Ibid.,* p. 188.

4. *Ibid.,* p. 189.

5. *Ibid.,* pp. 187–8. Freud remarked that this instance (with the subject's discussion of the situation in which it occurred, which amounted to "associations") almost "analyzed itself in the telling"; i.e., it was "distorted" only by a reversal in order of the two obsessional "commands" or "impulses," the first of which, to explain it, Freud expanded, "Kill yourself, as a punishment for these savage and murderous passions!" If the reversal was a "distortion," it seems probable not just that the whole train of thought was obscured by the subject's recognizing the two commands in reverse order, but also—as it was the "impulse" to murder another that was most repugnant, and over which he was guilty—that he was first trying to put it off by becoming aware, rather, of the responsive, self-punitive command.

6. In his summary of the Count Thun dream, Freud remembered that "the analysis of certain episodes in the dream showed them to be impertinent boastings, the issue of an absurd megalomania . . . which incidentally accounted for my exuberant spirits during the evening before I had the dream." (*The Interpretation of Dreams,* p. 215.) Freud was sufficiently averse to his "megalomania" as, apparently, to regard his public discussion of it as something of a sacrifice. However, the aversion to it was not so great as to outweigh the need for specimen dream-interpretations. For instance, see "dream of open air closet," pp. 468–9; "Count Thun dream," and his discussion of the preamble, pp. 201–18; the "dream of the botanical monograph," pp. 165, 169–76; the "dream of Otto looking ill," pp. 269–77; the "Rome series," pp. 194–6; the "dream of my uncle with yellow beard," pp. 135–45.

7. The patient reported a dream that her little nephew was lying dead in his coffin and gave the "association" that "the professor comes to see us again after a long absence." The patient's meaning for the dream-report indicated her love for the professor. Freud referred to the dream as one of impatience: she had in her pocket, while associating to the dream-report, a ticket to a concert at which she would be able to see the man she still loved. Sometimes this patient was fully aware of her love for the professor. She acknowledged it and discussed it, and she sometimes acted on it with full awareness that that was what she was doing, as when she bought tickets to lectures or concerts because she knew he would be there. On the other hand, she could regard a dream-report in its light, and in associating reveal and express it, without being aware that she was doing so. And she did not draw her own conclusion that the dream revealed this expectation and her love for him. She did, however, agree with Freud's conclusion to this effect. (*The Interpretation of Dreams,* pp. 152–4; also mentioned in pp. 189, 248, and 463.)

8. Probably any activity *could* be summed up in terms of "desire" and "satisfaction." But if one does apply this formula to every sort of activity, it becomes vacuous. Here is another example of the turning of recalcitrant material into wishes and fulfillments: Freud remarked to the Rat Man that "It was well known to us that patients derived a certain satisfaction from their sufferings, so that . . . they all resisted their recovery to a certain extent. He must never lose sight of the fact that a treatment like ours proceeded to the accompaniment of a *constant resistance* . . ." (*Two Case Histories,* pp. 183–4; Freud's italics). Freud's cases show that there is a better explanation for the fact of "resistance" than the patients' putative pleasure in their suffering; that is, that they want not to know of the emotions that explain their symptoms.

9. And the second-level interpretation mentioned here in summary style (it will be further considered) is not to be equated with the final report on the Rat Man and his symptoms, or on this symptom.

10. And said so, in effect, long before he became fully aware that he did maintain a rage against his father. (E.g., *Two Case Histories,* p. 183.)

11. E.g., *The Interpretation of Dreams,* p. 556; p. 580 and note.

12. Freud himself seems now to regard this view as a literally correct account, now as an empirical hypothesis, again as a scientific fiction, and again as a metaphor or picture-story, or a version of the (more correct) quantity-process view of the two processes that is suitable for presentation to popular audiences.

13. *The Interpretation of Dreams,* p. 570.

14. *Two Case Histories,* pp. 198–9.

15. *Ibid.,* pp. 165–73; 210–20.

16. E.g., *Two Case Histories,* p. 112.

CHAPTER 5

1. *Two Case Histories,* p. 174.

2. *Ibid.,* pp. 178–9.

3. *Ibid.,* p. 182.

4. *Ibid.,* p. 182. I have introduced these few instances only in order to indicate, in a general way, the sort of relationships among emotions and conceptions that Freud was finding, and the way in which he found them; of course there were many more instances taken into account. I should make clear that the way in which the preliminary interpretations are brought together toward a progressively clearer and firmer set of conclusions about the subject, and the general direction of the inquiry—the ends to which Freud is steering—require to be drawn out from his reports. In the first place, these are inexplicit, or at least not emphatically presented; in the second place, they are obscured by theoretical asides, manners of statement, and aims. For example, the series mentioned above is presented in the context of a very general discussion between Freud and the patient of psychoanalytic theory. In connection

with point A, Freud discussed "displacement" ("when there is a *mésalliance,* I began, between an affect and its ideational content . . ." p. 175); he did not until later (p. 201) explicitly point out the relation between points A and B, and the tentative conclusion that the Rat Man's "obsessive thoughts" had amounted to, or included, wishes for his father's death looks at first as if it were based only on the "unmistakable indication of an opposition between the two objects of his love" (p. 179) in the obsessions—one in particular—and on the patient's repudiation of the "thoughts" and his guilt over them. Freud did not present a case history as the story of a search for a pattern underlying the recurrence of relations among emotions and conceptions, and he quite regularly made his general conclusions seem less soundly based than they were. He would say, for instance, "Starting from these indications and from other data of a similar kind, I ventured to put forth a construction . . ." (p. 205); one might wonder what the "other data" were, but in fact the "construction," or something very like it, was based upon the convergence of all the data that had been mentioned to that point.

5. *Ibid.,* p. 183. To Freud, this further repetition of motifs in pattern—with the subject's explicit comparison of himself to the woman and his statement that he deserved to die for his "thoughts"—virtually confirmed the hypothesis, but it did not do so for the Rat Man.

6. *Ibid.,* pp. 187–9.

7. *Ibid.,* pp. 190–2.

8. *Ibid.,* pp. 198–9. On the other hand, Freud considered the patient's recent and severe outbreak of neurosis a reaction to his father's death (p. 235). The question of "exciting cause" will be considered in the next chapter.

9. *Ibid.,* pp. 203–4. The story was in *Dichtung und Wahrheit.*

10. *Ibid.,* pp. 205–6.

11. *Ibid.,* p. 201. That the ingredients previously discerned as focal points in the Rat Man's world fell into one pattern or structure in terms of his memory of his last beating tended clearly to confirm Freud's hypothesis.

12. Freud presents his "sexual instinct" (with its component-impulses or instincts, as oral, anal, sadistic, scopophilic) as something mediating or bridging a gap between physiological processes (or somatic excitation) and pleasure-seeking desires, tendencies (dispositions), and activities, or what he calls the "aims and objects," that is, sensually-desired activities and partners, or the parts of one's own or another's body that are sought for sensual pleasure. By their aims (and objects) alone, he said, we know the instincts: otherwise they are unobservable. ("Instincts and their Vicissitudes," Vol. XIV, p. 123. In "The Unconscious" he remarked that unless an instinct attaches itself to an idea or is manifested in an affective state, we know nothing about it, p. 177.) His account of the *Triebe* as excitation (the psychical representatives of processes of somatic excitation, themselves having psychical representatives in ideas) is incoherent, and he gives no less questionable or more coherent picture of the instincts as something between or other than somatic processes, and desires and acts—or aims and objects. In practice, the "instincts" function as general titles holding together groups of (organ-) pleasure-seeking desires and activities, with other desires, activities, tendencies, and emotions not directly sensual, and asserting relationships among them of similarity or sequence. That is, the "instincts" can be considered as a system for classifying sexual, proto-sexual, and ex-sexual (sublimated) tendencies, desires, and activities.

13. This is not to say that there is nothing sexual in cases of neurosis as Freud interprets them; sexual/erotic desires or emotions have some part in all the conflicts in terms of which he interprets neurotics.

14. In the case of the Wolf Man Freud treated as of greatest importance in his investigation two childhood memories: one of an event (probably modified by fantasy) and the other of a dream; together they epitomized a structure of beliefs and emotions of which the central ingredients were the subject's erotic love of his father and his belief that in order to enjoy love of his father he would have to be castrated. A part of his

adult neurosis was interpreted in terms of the conflict between (homo)sexual desire and fear of castration. In Hans' case, Freud placed emphasis on a recent event, which he considered not as a predisposing, but as an "exciting" cause, but it was similar to the events in the other cases in that it illustrated (indirectly) the conflicting beliefs and emotions in terms of which the subject's phobia was interpreted—in sum, semierotic love of his mother with jealousy toward his father, and fear of the results of these emotions. It may be noted that attachment to "Oedipal objects" plays a central part in neurotic conflicts as Freud found them in his cases—and not only in cases of hysteria, which was theoretically accounted for in terms of fixation to (of, at) Oedipal objects and regressions to that point of fixation—but the emotions and desires in question do not need and cannot use the theory of instincts for elucidation, and (as will become clearer in the next chapter) to submit them to the formula of fixation, repression, and regression is to obscure them and the place they have in neurotic conflicts.

15. Freud states (in the *Introductory Lectures,* Vol. XVI, pp. 343–4) that in obsessional neurosis, "It is the regression of the libido to the preliminary stage of the sadistic-anal organization that is the most striking fact and the one which is decisive for what is manifested in symptoms. The love-impulse is obliged, when this has happened, to disguise itself as a sadistic impulse. The obsessional idea 'I should like to kill you,' when it has been freed from certain additions which are not a matter of chance but are indispensible [?], means at bottom nothing more than 'I should like to enjoy you in love.'" "Regression" will be dealt with in the next chapter.

16. *A Case of Obsessional Neurosis,* p. 213.

17. *Ibid.,* p. 240. Freud's restraint in the whole of this discussion as to the part played in neurosis by the instincts is in marked contrast to some of his formulations: cf. the passage quoted above (note 15). Dora, a hysteric, sounds more of a "sadist" than Freud's obsessional neurotics: the Wolf Man had had a sadistic phase in which he pulled butterflies apart and the like, but it was not shown to have been a pre-

cursor to the ingredients of his central conflict. (He had also been oral-incorporative or "cannibal," masochistic, phallic, scopophilic, homosexually and heterosexually genital, anal-erotic, etc.)

18. *Ibid.*, pp. 217–8.

19. *Ibid.*, pp. 215–8; see also *Introductory Lectures*, p. 315 and note.

20. *A Case of Obsessional Neurosis*, p. 238.

21. And it is not just a conflict between hatred and love; it could at least as well be called a conflict between, or rather among, beliefs.

22. Freud's reference to the repression of the subject's hatred for his father as the decisive "event" in the development of the neurosis seems, judging from his report of the case, to be misleading both in its isolation of that emotion as alone "pathogenic" and in its assumption that the repression of such an emotion is an event, or occurs upon an occasion (while, if other "ideas" are unconscious, they need not be thought to have become so on an event). Similar assumptions, with their theoretical background, were discussed in Chapter II above. The Rat Man's own statement that he "became a coward" after and presumably as a result of his last beating has to be considered. Perhaps he meant that because of the event (because of being beaten or because of his own extremely angry response?) he came to have an excessive fear of violence (probably, on the part of others and himself). Fear of the possible results of his own rage, and also fear of further punishment, were in opposition to his hostility to his father and among his reasons for wanting not to know about it, but this does not indicate that from that day forward he was unconscious of hostility toward his father. It does not seem very likely either, despite the patient's opinion, than an excessive fear of violence could be attributed to the one experience. It is to be noted that the memory was central *for him;* he used it as a focus of various fantasies.

23. The hostility could in a sense be explained in terms of the subject's belief that his father was opposed to his erotic satisfac-

tion and that to satisfy erotic desires would be to disobey his father and to provoke punishment from him. The problem is then to account for the beliefs. Although the patient's memory of the event (in his version) illustrates these beliefs, it does not seem that one beating can account for his holding them, especially his holding them very firmly. Similarly, his wanting not to know about his hostility (and the remainder of the constellation) can be at least partially explained in terms of the beliefs that his rage was hateful and dangerous to himself and his father; again, the memory illustrates these beliefs, but a boy's once frightening himself by falling into a rage does not seem sufficient to instill such beliefs in him.

24. Freud, as usual emphasizing the hostility, noted in effect that it could not be accounted for in terms of the father's general character or general treatment of his son: "from all accounts," the man was an excellent, companionable, affectionate father and an admirable, humorous, forthright person, although he was occasionally "hasty and violent" in punishing his children when they were "young and naughty" (*A Case of Obsessional Neurosis,* pp. 200–1). In such a case it is at least tempting to fall back for explanation on the subject's innate constitution (or phylogenesis); but although in the most general way it seems likely that there are constitutional factors at work, none in particular are demonstrated.

25. No one would expect to be able to account for most ordinary preconceptions and/or "chronic emotions" in terms of specific experiences or specifiable aspects of the subject's constitution, even if they could vaguely be traced back to his childhood, or if the subject's view of the nature of their origin were summed up in his memories of childhood. There may, of course, be something known about a person's history that makes it *understandable* that he *does* hold particular beliefs—in the interpretation of neurosis as well as in ordinary cases.

26. For the most recent, see Jeffrey Masson, *Assault on Truth* (New York: Penguin, 1987).

27. For example, although he was inclined to accept the Rat

175

Man's mother's version of the beating as more probably factually correct than the patient's, because she was an adult at the time the event occurred, he certainly did not leave out of consideration that part of the subject's version that did not agree with his mother's; he was more concerned to pursue the ramifications of (obvious) fantasy that the subject built up around the event than to determine the evidential value of either version (*A Case of Obsessional Neurosis*, pp. 206–7). Freud justified his continuing emphasis on childhood "experiences" after it became clear that many of the important events in patients' childhoods had not in fact happened on the ambiguous ground that the false or partly false memories possessed "psychical reality," and that *"in the world of the neuroses it is psychical reality which is the decisive kind"* (*Introductory Lectures,* p. 368). Thus he seemed to be retaining the causal link between childhood event and adult conflict (sometimes, via the "mnemic image" that might be laid down by fantasy as well as by actual "experiences of satisfaction"); but at the same time he was almost explicitly stating, and certainly implying, that for this investigation what is in question is what the subject believes and feels, and not what can account for his beliefs and feelings: "It remains a fact that the patient has created these phantasies for himself, and this fact is of scarcely less importance for his neurosis than if he had really experienced what the phantasies contain" (*Ibid.*).

28. *Two Case Histories,* p. 207.

29. Although, in the theoretical discussion that followed the case history proper of the Rat Man, Freud made some effort to introduce what might seem a simpler or prior structure—in terms of instincts—he added nothing to contradict this statement.

30. Such a memory as the Rat Man's of his last beating does not in itself demonstrate that the constellation of beliefs and emotions is as old as the event, since the memory may only later have come to sum up at once the subject's central unconscious beliefs and emotions and his view of that to which they respond. But there were some indications that these conflicting

176

beliefs and emotions were established in the Rat Man's childhood, such as the obsessions he had as a young boy, the interpretation of which helped to lead to the discovery of the memory, and, with all the other material, showed the memory as important.

31. *Two Case Histories,* p. 209.

32. *Ibid.*

33. This language of "constellation" and "pattern" or "structure," and talk of the neurotic's state of mind or his conflicting attitudes as capable of being regarded as made up of such and such (specified) beliefs, emotions, and desires may be misleading in that it may seem to represent the neurotic state of mind as more clear-cut, sharply definable, and, in one sense, logical than it is. The neurotic structure of thought is vague, elusive, tenuous, and, of course, no structure in any quasi-architectural sense. The neurotic's state of mind cannot be broken down into so many distinct, countable "units" of belief and emotion, such as (one might imagine) could be "taken out" and examined one by one.

CHAPTER 6

1. "I consider that these unconscious wishes are always on the alert, ready at any time to find their way to expression when an opportunity arises for allying themselves with an impulse from the conscious and for transferring their own great intensity on to the latter's lesser one. They share this character of indestructibility with all mental acts which are truly unconscious, i.e., which belong to the system *Ucs.* only. These are paths which have been laid down once and for all, which never fall into disuse and which, whenever an unconscious excitation re-cathects them, are always ready to conduct the excitatory process to discharge." (*Interpretation of Dreams,* Vol. V, p. 553 and note.) "Indeed it is a prominent feature of unconscious processes that they are indestructible. In the unconscious noth-

ing can be brought to an end, nothing is past or forgotten"
(p. 577).

2. "And indeed the whole rebellious content of the dream
[of Count Thun] with its *lese majeste* and its derision of the
higher authorities, went back to rebellion against my father."
(*Interpretation of Dreams,* Vol. IV, p. 217n.) But the "content"
of the dream-report was not rebellious, and the "content" of
the dream-report did not go back to rebellion against his father; Freud makes quite clear in this discussion that what
went back to rebellion against his father was his general rebelliousness, or assessment of himself as more worthy than
the public worthies, which he expressed in a meaning for the
dream-report.

3. *Interpretation of Dreams.* Probably, if he had set out to
express or state his attitude toward his father, instead of indirectly expressing it through his "associations" to a dream, he
would have stated it at least partly in the past tense.

4. If I am right in drawing out what Freud's interpretations
imply, in either case—Freud's or the Rat Man's—the contemporary attitude may be accounted for in terms of the old one,
in the sense that, had the subject not, for instance, learned
pride and defiance at his father's knee, he would not now be so
likely to regard official and/or privileged personages with the
expectation of finding evidences of their lack of worthiness to
be set above himself—which, being on the look-out for, he
easily finds. In either case, in this respect at least, the primitive
attitude is prior to the present one. In either case, too, the contemporary version is what, however unclearly, first strikes
the subject. Part of the point above is that the two kinds of
case can be distinguished on the ground that something like
the Rat Man's habit of regarding people as frustrating him, and
himself as guilty for his consequent rage against them, unlike
Freud's habit of regarding himself as greater than others, can
be almost wholly accounted for in terms of his fundamental
structure of thought: there is always something to hang his
attitudes on, so to speak (though seldom any close approach to
what would be understood as an occasion for them), but he can

be said just to be going about viewing "reality" as reflecting (realizing, re-presenting) his primary beliefs, and it is these which he mostly has in mind. But in the other case, the contemporary attitude is accounted for by a primitive one only in the sense just mentioned. And it seems likely that in Freud's case, it is only that the contemporary attitude has called up or in effect reminded the subject of the childhood one, which otherwise he would be unlikely to have in mind or be expressing or acting on.

5. See, for instance, *Interpretation of Dreams,* especially pp. 614–5; *Introductory Lectures,* especially pp. 294–6; *The Question of Lay Analysis,* Vol. XX, pp. 197–8; "The Unconscious," Vol. XIV.

6. See the second, third, and fourth chapters above.

7. See note 7 in Chapter IV.

8. See note 6 in Chapter IV.

9. "The Unconscious," Vol. XIV, p. 177.

10. *Notes upon a Case of Obsessional Neurosis,* Vol. X, p. 158.

11. Obviously, "not knowing" is not always "not wanting to know." Freud was constantly making clear through his interpretations that he was not talking about the unconscious, but about that which was inexplicit, unformulated, indirectly expressed and acted on, and seen as realized, because the subject preferred not, or wanted not, to know about it. It has been asked why the Freudian "unconscious" should be so unpleasant; sometimes with the implication that the unpleasantness is in the minds of Freud and the Freudians. Again, what is unconscious in the "ordinary" sense is not what one would rather not or must not know about in oneself and so it need not be weak, ignoble, embarrassing, or vile and frightful; but where "not knowing" is "not wanting to know," what is "unconscious" must, at least in the subject's view, be at least dislikable in himself.

12. The comparison between Freud's and the Rat Man's primitive beliefs and emotions indicates the invalidity of one of the implications of Freud's theoretical view of "the unconscious": i.e., that the "core of our being," the leftover, "infantile" ma-

terial, is all of a kind, and is in every case equally unavailable to consciousness or equally "unconscious" (and that the fundamental "unconscious" in neurotics differs from that in non-neurotics mainly, at least, in "amount" or "force"). Freud held in theory that all "dreams" could ultimately be "interpreted" in terms of fundamental "unconscious, infantile wishes." It is impossible to tell whether all or most dream-reports might be given a further level of meaning in terms of "trains of thought leading back to childhood," or whether further-level dream-constructions, if they were made, would regularly be found to reveal attitudes toward the central figures of the subject's childhood—such as Freud's "rebellious" attitude toward his father, or the Rat Man's hostile attitude toward his father. But the present point shows that, supposing they did, the further level of meaning would not therefore be very different from the first in some cases: Freud, who no more than disapproved of his primitive rebellion or "megalomania," could make out a dream as meaning something that would, if the case, be satisfying to it, without having to make it out also to mean something dreadful. The Wolf Man, however, when he constructed as the meaning for a dream-report that the sexual activity he wanted, but greatly feared, was available, had to make out the report as meaning also, and most prominently, a threat of castration. In the one case the further-level beliefs and emotions are, perhaps, a degree more reprehensible and to be avoided than the first-level attitudes; in the other case, the further-level beliefs and emotions are in conflict such that the subject cannot even make out a dream-report as meaning something that would satisfy the most frightful of them without also making it out to mean something that would greatly dissatisfy himself.

13. Compare the episode of the old woman, in which the Rat Man's getting a razor to cut his throat could be seen as (a) a gesture toward punishing himself for his murderous rage at the lady's grandmother, and (b) an attempt to keep that rage at bay: he would sooner be aware of an "impulse" to kill himself. (The distraction failed in this instance at the point when the Rat Man had the razor at his throat.)

14. "On the Psychical Mechanism of Hysterical Phenomena" in *Standard Edition,* Vol. III, pp. 31–2.

15. If the view of symptoms as smoke screens is correct, then the "manifest content" is a "substitute" or even a "cover" for the "latent"; but it is not something that the subject takes as a distorted satisfaction, but something he throws up (or stresses as "manifest content") in order to distort (prevent, avoid, deny, repudiate) what it means to him.

SELECTED
BIBLIOGRAPHY

Freud develops the inherent logic in Freud using *The Standard Edition of the Complete Psychological Works of Sigmund Freud,* 24 vols., revised and edited by James Strachey, in collaboration with Anna Freud, assisted by Alix Strachey and Alan Tyson (London: Hogarth Press and the Institute of Psycho-Analysis, 1953–77). The following is a selected list of books and articles which develop or criticize differing aspects of Freud and his ideas.

CRITICISMS OF THE STRACHEY TRANSLATION

Bettelheim, Bruno. *Freud and Man's Soul.* New York: Vintage, 1984. More a statement about Bettelheim's concerns than Strachey's translation. See Peter Gay's comment (*Freud: A Life of Our Time,* p. 749) on his evaluation of Bettelheim's conclusions about the Strachey translation.

Mahony, Patrick. *Psychoanalysis and Discourse.* N.p.: Tavistock Publications, 1987. Points out that Freud's vibrancy, ambiguity, and "his polyphonic for of expression" are lost in the Strachey translation.

INTERPRETATIVE BIOGRAPHIES

Gay, Peter. *Freud: A Life of Our Time*. New York: Norton, 1988. A brilliant work integrating what is known about Freud. See Gay's bibliographical essay (pp. 741–91) for an exhaustive account of the available literature.

Jones, Ernest. *Life and Work of Sigmund Freud*, 3 vols. New York: Basic Books; London: Hogarth Press, 1953–57. In my mind, for many reasons, notwithstanding all of its known shortcomings, still the best.

Wollheim, Richard. *Freud*. 1971. Reprint. New York: Cambridge University Press, 1977. Short, compact, excellent.

THE CORRESPONDENCE OF FREUD

Abraham, Hilda, and Freud, Ernst, eds. *A Psychoanalytic Dialogue: The Letters of Sigmund Freud and Karl Abraham, 1907–1926*. Translated by Bernard Marsh and Hilda Abraham. New York: Basic Books; London: Hogarth Press and the Institute of Psycho-Analysis, 1965.

Freud, Ernst, ed. *Letters of Sigmund Freud*. Translated by Tania and James Stern. New York: Basic Books; London: Hogarth Press, 1961.

Freud, Ernst, and Meng, Heinrich, eds. *Psychoanalysis and Faith: The Letters of Sigmund Freud and Oskar Phister*. Translated by Eric Mossbacher. New York: Basic Books; London: Hogarth Press and the Institute of Psycho-Analysis, 1963.

Masson, Jeffrey, ed. *The Complete Letters of Sigmund Freud to Wilhelm Fliess*. Cambridge: Harvard University Press, Belknap Press, 1986.

McGuire, William, ed. *The Freud/Jung Letters: The Correspondence between Sigmund Freud and C.G. Jung*. Translated by Ralph Manheim and R.F.C. Hull. Princeton, NJ: Princeton University Press; London: Routledge and Kegan Paul, 1974.

Pheiffer, Ernst, ed. *Sigmund Freud and Lou Andreas-Salome: Let-*

ters. Translated by William and Elaine Robson-Scott. New York: Harcourt Brace Jovanovich; London: Hogarth Press and the Institute of Psycho-Analysis, 1972.

SOME CRITICAL, INTERPRETATIVE, MATERIAL

Hook, Sidney. *Psychoanalysis, Scientific Method and Philosophy*. New York: Grove Press, 1960. What can happen when one thinks Freud is, or is not, offering an explanation that models that given in the natural sciences.

MacIntyre, A.C. *The Unconscious*. Boston: Routledge and Kegan Paul, 1958. Tries to solve confusions in Freud by distinguishing motives from causes. Oversimplified, but makes one think.

Masson, Jeffrey. *The Assault on Truth: Freud's Suppression of the Seduction Theory*. New York: Farrar, Straus and Giroux, 1984. A serious misunderstanding of why Freud was forced to make changes in his seduction theory.

Peters, R.S. *The Concept of Motivation*. Boston: Routledge and Kegan Paul, 1958. Same type of approach as MacIntyre with different conclusions about Freud's theory and type of explanation.

Riciour, Paul. *Freud and Philosophy: An Essay on Interpretation*. Translated by Denis Savage. New Haven, CT: Yale University Press, 1970. Similar concerns as *Freud* but takes a different route leading to opposite conclusions. Very provocative.

Robert, Marthe. *From Oedipus to Moses*. Translated by Ralph Manheim. New York: Vintage, 1976. Influence of Jewish tradition on Freud.

Sartre, J.P. *Existential Psychoanalysis*. N.p.: Gateway, 1953. A selection from *Being and Nothingness* that shines a light on Freud's thinking.

Schafer, Roy. *New Language for Psychoanalysis*. New Haven, CT: Yale University Press, 1976. From a totally different perspective, *Freud* supports many of Schafer's positions.

Schur, Max. *Freud Living and Dying*. New York: International Universities Press; London: Hogarth Press and the Institute of Psycho-Analysis, 1972. Insights from Freud's physician and friend.

Sulloway, Frank J. *Freud: Biologist of the Mind*. New York: Basic Books, 1979. Driving the biological nail home with a jackhammer, but still interesting.

Wachtel, Paul. *Psychoanalysis and Behavior Therapy*. New York: Basic Books, 1977. Brings out views that *Freud* supports. Especially, neurosis in terms of "cyclical patterns."

Wollheim, Richard, ed. *Freud: A Collection of Critical Essays*. New York: Doubleday, Anchor Press, 1974. Some excellent essays.

ON THE RAT MAN

Mahony, Patrick. *Freud and the Rat Man*. New Haven, CT: Yale University Press, 1986. A psychoanalytic reinterpretation using some of the process notes that were not published in the *Standard Edition*.

Schneiderman, Stuart. *Rat Man*. New York: New York University Press, 1986. More about Lacan than the Rat Man. Interesting.

INDEX

Hysteria (*cont.*)
    excitation concepts in,
        5–8, 15–16, 20
    strangulation and abreaction
        of affective ideas and,
        11–15
Hysterical counter-will, 151

Id, 165 n.17
    as first agency, 75–76, 96
Idea
    affect associated with, 7, 9
        (*see also* Affective idea)
    desires and, 162 n.40
    levels of consciousness of,
        36, 133–143, 161 n.29
    pathogenic, 25–26
    quantity of affect and, 19
    split off from consciousness,
        9–10
Infantile wishes, 47, 57–58, 69
    dreams and, 73–74
Instinct, 65, 164–165 n.16
    sexual, 60, 116, 162 n.40, 172
        n.12
Interpretation of Dreams, The,
        3–4, 46, 51, 52, 53, 54, 55,
        73

Latent content
    of symptoms, 96
    of thoughts, 63–64
Libido theory, 45, 53, 59–60
    cathexis of ideas in, 162 n.40,
        164 n.16
    classification of desires in, 65
    fixation in, 116

Manifest content
    of dream, 63–64, 74
    of symptoms, 85, 96
Megalomania, 90, 131–132,
        135, 143, 168 n.6, 178 n.2,
        180 n.12
Memory of events
    associated with affect, 7, 9
    child's, and adult thought
        patterns, 114–118
    conflicts discovered through,
        29–30, 33–34
    split off from consciousness,
        9–10
    traumatic events, 40–41
Memory-trace, 18, 56
Mental apparatus, 52–54
    wish-fulfillment theory and,
        56–57, 73
Mental processes, 41
Mistaking-for case in neurotics,
        86
Mnemic images, 72, 175–176
        n.27
Mobility, theory of, 13, 14–15,
        88–93
Motor innervation, 8, 88, 159
        n.11

Neurological explanations of
        symptoms, 41–50
Neuron, excitation of, 41–42
"Neuro-Psychoses of Defense,
        The," 4, 17, 18
Neurosis, 4, 17–18. *See also*
        Symptom(s)
    meaning of, in conflict
        theory, 154–155

Rat Man case (*cont.*)
  relationship with father and
    erotic frustration in,
    94–95, 99, 101, 106,
    111–114, 115–125, 174
    n.22, 174 n.23, 175 n.24
  responding-to emotion in,
    86–88, 92
  seeing-as emotion in, 92
  self-anger and suicidal
    impulses in, 83–85, 87,
    91–92, 101–102, 112, 113,
    171 n.5
  substitution of rage in,
    90–93, 101–102
  unconsciousness in, 134–135,
    142–143, 149–150,
    179–180 n.12
Reaction. *See* Emotional
  reaction
Reality
  neurotic's view of, 131–132,
    148, 178–179 n.4
  principle of, 57, 76
Repression, theory of, 20–21,
    162 n.40
  in case of Elisabeth von R.,
    24–26, 104
  disintegration of affect
    through repression, 45–46
Resistance, 1, 23, 36, 169 n.8
  defense and, 27–29
  melting, 30–34
  unconscious, 26–30,
    140–141, 147
Responding-to cases in
  neurotics, 85–88
  substitution and, 89

Sadism, 117–121, 172 n.12, 173
  n.15, 173–174 n.17
Satisfaction
  denial of, to neurotics by
    symptoms, 91–93, 95–96,
    100–105
  relief from excitation as, 48
  substitution and, 89–93
Seeing-as case in neurotics,
    85–88, 89, 92, 145
Self-anger, case of Rat Man,
    83–85, 87, 91–92,
    101–102, 112, 113, 171 n.5
Self-deprivation, 101
Self-distraction, 38
Self-punishment, case of
    Elisabeth von R., 38
Sexual instinct, 60, 116, 162
    n.40, 172 n.12
Somatic innervation, 19, 20
Strangulated affect, 9, 11,
    12–13, 17
Studies of Hysteria, 4, 5, 51
Substitution of affect, 88–95,
    101–102
  displacement and, 19, 21
  responding-to and, 89, 92
Substitutive gratification,
    theory of, 89–91, 151–152
Suicidal impulses in case of Rat
    Man, 83–85, 87, 91–92,
    101, 111, 112, 171 n.5
Summation of traumas, 40, 41
Sum of effect, 6, 7, 19
Symptom(s). *See also* Thought
    patterns and symptoms
  as abnormal expression of
    emotion, 9–10, 17, 159 n.11

conflict and, 37–38
developed from traumatic event, 27
dreams and neurotic, 52, 53, 163 n.4
exciting causes of, 145–146
factors involved in interpretation of, 164 n.16
formation of neurotic, 57–60, 62–65, 69–70
neurological explanations of, 41–50
patterns of thought developing around, 147–152
as smoke screen, 150
substantial beliefs and, 144–145
unconsciousness and, 143–144, 147

Symptoms, Freud's preliminary interpretations of, 82–108
compromise-gratification theory and, 95–105
conflict in neurotics and, 105–108
introduction to Rat Man case, 83–85
seeing-as or responding-to in neurotics and, 85–88
substitution in neurotics and, 88–95

"Talking cure," 8–9
Theory, relationship of case material to Freud's, 1–2

Therapist
role of, 14
transference of emotions to, 126
Thought patterns and symptoms, 109–128
childhood memory and, 114–128
delineating, in Rat Man case, 110–114
not wanting to know linked to, 144, 146, 148–149
shortcomings of wish-fulfillment theory and, 109–110
Transference
concept of, 39
to therapist, 126
of thoughts, 58–59, 79
of wishes, 38
Traumatic events
in Elisabeth von R. case, 40–41
in Rat Man case, 115–116, 122, 124, 175–176 n.27
split-off memory of, 9
symptoms developed from, 27–28

Unconscious, 43
as first agency, 75, 79, 96
Unconsciousness, ideas and levels of consciousness and, 36, 133–143, 161 n.29, 178–179 n.4
Unconscious system (System Ucs.), 57, 58, 67–71, 74–76, 133, 161 n.38